This book is a gift to:

_____

From:

_____

Date:

_____

Life Is Beautiful

Previously published under the title *Simply Refreshing*

© 2008 Christian Art Gifts, RSA
Christian Art Gifts Inc., IL, USA

Second edition © 2013

Designed by Christian Art Gifts

Images used under license from Shutterstock.com

Printed in China

ISBN 978-1-4321-0526-6

13 14 15 16 17 18 19 20 21 22 – 13 12 11 10 9 8 7 6 5 4

One-Minute Devotions

Life Is Beautiful

Cherish each day

Ellen Banks Elwell

christian
art gifts®

January

God Is Everywhere

If I ride the wings of the morning, if I dwell by the farthest oceans, even there Your hand will guide me, and Your strength will support me.

Psalm 139:9-10

If we could actually do what the psalmist suggests and ride the wings of the morning to the farthest oceans, we might end up in Fiji. Situated directly east of the north coast of Australia, Fiji is made up of about 300 beautiful islands.

Because the International Date Line passes between some of these islands, Fiji is one of the first countries in the world to welcome each new day.

Most of us won't have the opportunity to visit these islands, but if we did, God would be every bit as present there as He is anywhere else in the world. We can experience the love of God and the comfort of His presence no matter where we are. He is present everywhere.

Father,
We're grateful that Your strength and guidance are always available, ready to refresh us wherever we may be. Amen.

January 1

All of It

All Scripture is inspired by God and is useful to teach us what is true and to make us realize what is wrong in our lives. It corrects us when we are wrong and teaches us to do what is right. God uses it to prepare and equip His people to do every good work.

2 Timothy 3:16-17

The apostle Paul began these verses with the little word *all*. "All Scripture is inspired by God and is useful." The Bible tells one story from start to finish. It opens in a garden, closes in a city, and all the way through points to Jesus. We learn about God, ourselves, sin, how God reaches out to us, and how He provided His Son, Jesus, as the way for us to know Him.

The Bible equips us to deal with our struggles. It helps us to gain new perspective, because we see heaven ahead of us. What a rich experience it is to immerse ourselves in the Bible – all of it!

Father,
The gift of Your Word makes us rich. May we value all of it.
Amen.

January 2

Walk with God

Noah found favor with the Lord. Noah was a righteous man, the only blameless person living on earth at the time, and he walked in close fellowship with God.

Genesis 6:8-9

Noah wasn't perfect. The Bible makes that clear. Nonetheless, he was righteous and he walked with God. All throughout the Bible, walking is much more than physically putting one foot in front of the other. Walking signifies relationship. Where a person was headed and who they chose to walk with made all the difference in the world.

Over the long years (it took 120 years to build the ark), Noah walked closely with God and was commended for his faith, obedience, and righteousness (Heb. 11:7). How delightful it would be if, at the end of our lives, others could say about us, "She walked with God."

Father,
We long to be close to You and to sense Your favor, just like Noah. Help us to walk with You each day. Amen.

January 3

A Mansion Beyond

*"There is more than enough room in My Father's home.
When everything is ready, I will come and get you, so that
you will always be with Me where I am."*

John 14:2-3

Situated on 17 acres in Provence, France, is a stately mansion that rents for $50,000 a week. With 16 bedrooms and 16 bathrooms, there's plenty of space for the whole family! Situated in heaven, with more than enough room, are large and stately mansions for us to live in forever. Jesus paid the price for us to stay there. He paid with His blood because He wants us to be able to live with Him for eternity. Our entrance is secured by our faith in Him.

While we may eagerly look forward to our earthly vacations – be they camping or luxury resorts – nothing can be compared to the lavish wonders of our heavenly home. Our holidays may seem to end too quickly but heaven will be our new home, and it will be a place of unending rest and delight!

January 4

Lord,
Thank You that I have so much to look forward to. Help me not to lose sight of the beautiful future You have for me. Amen.

Greater Than ...

You belong to God, my dear children. You have already won a
victory over those people, because the Spirit who lives in you
is greater than the spirit who lives in the world.

1 John 4:4

Do you remember the greater than (>) less than (<)
mathematical symbols we learned back in school?
None of us would ever argue that five is not greater
than three, or that one is not less than four. That's
obvious. Sometimes, though, the 'greater than, less
than' principle looks more obvious to us in the mathematical realm than it does in the spiritual realm.

Lest we as God's children forget, the apostle
John reminds us that God's Spirit is greater than any
fears or temptations we could ever face. No matter
what challenges or difficulties we are dealing with
today, the Spirit who lives in us is greater than the
spirit who lives in the world.

Father,
Even at times when it doesn't seem obvious to us, help us to
believe that Your Spirit is greater than the spirit of the world.
Amen.

Free Food

*"Is anyone thirsty? Come and drink – even if you
have no money! Come, take your choice of wine or milk –
it's all free! Why spend your money on food that does
not give you strength? Listen to Me, and you will eat
what is good. You will enjoy the finest food."*

Isaiah 55:1-2

If you travel to Austria and order Wiener schnitzel for dinner, take some euros to pay for the meal. If you visit India and opt for Chicken Tandori, make sure that you put some rupee in your wallet. Regardless of where we eat, food costs money.

When Jesus invites everyone in the whole world to enjoy His gospel feast, He tells us that we don't need any money. All He asks is that we come to Him with a sense of our need – with thirsty hearts.

In return for our longing, He blesses us with the free gift of His grace and lasting nourishment from His presence and His Word.

Gracious Father,
How kind of You to make the finest food available to us all –
with no money required. Amen.

January 6

God Satisfies

He is the God who made the world and everything in it.
Since He is Lord of heaven and earth, He doesn't live in
man-made temples, and human hands can't serve His
needs – for He has no needs. He Himself gives life and
breath to everything, and He satisfies every need.
Acts 17:24-25

Imagine if we were completely satisfied and did not have any needs. No need for food ... sleep ... water ... money ... forgiveness. With no needs of our own, we would be entirely free to concentrate on other people's needs. Actually, that is what God is doing right now. He is taking care of our needs.

The One who created food at the beginning of the world still provides it today. The One who sent His Son to provide forgiveness of sins still provides it today. God didn't bring us into existence only to leave us on our own. Instead, He demonstrates His love continually by caring for our needs.

Gracious Father,
We are grateful for the many ways You show Your care for us.
Amen.

January 7

God Hears and Helps

As for me, I look to the LORD for help. I wait confidently
for God to save me, and my God will certainly hear me.
Micah 7:7

Great faith isn't just limited to the prophets. The faith of the Old Testament prophet, Micah, can be ours as well. Look to the Lord for help. More than taking a peek or a glance at God, we make Him the center of our attention. He becomes our Pole Star as we read His Word, think about Him, and talk to Him.

I wait confidently for God to save me. Sometimes we think of waiting in terms of standing in line, but waiting can be more purposeful than that. We can pray, linger in God's Word, and watch for His goodness. Our faith will grow as we look at our challenges in the light of God's power instead of looking at God in the shadow of our challenges. He will help us.

Father,
What would we do without You? Thank You for hearing us, helping us, and saving us. Amen.

January 8

Precious Wisdom

Wisdom is more precious than rubies;
nothing you desire can compare with her.
Proverbs 3:15

Just how precious are rubies? Along with diamonds, emeralds, and sapphires, they are considered one of the four precious gems and are exceptionally rare. Not found just anywhere, rubies are unearthed most often in Burma, Sri-Lanka, Kenya, Madagascar and Cambodia. If we were to purchase one of these gems to be set in a ring or hung on a necklace, we might pay anywhere from $500 to $5,000 for the piece of jewelry.

Wisdom is even more valuable than rubies, and we don't need to travel to Asia, Africa, or our local jeweler to find it. Wisdom is unearthed in God's Word, with the help of His Holy Spirit. The only tools we need to acquire it are a Bible and a receptive heart.

Father,
We're thankful that we have constant access to Your wisdom.
Amen.

January 9

A Staggering Debt

*"Therefore, the kingdom of heaven is like a king who
wanted to settle accounts with his servants.
As he began the settlement, a man who owed him ten
thousand talents was brought to him. The servant fell on his
knees before him. 'Be patient with me', he begged,
'and I will pay back everything'. The servant's master took
pity on him, canceled the debt and let him go."*
Matthew 18:23-24; 26-27 (NIV)

Jesus' parable about forgiveness means significantly more to us when we understand the amounts of money being discussed. The servant in this parable owed the master 10,000 talents.

In the first century, *one* talent was equivalent to a worker's wages for about 15 years. This meant that the servant owed his master 150,000 years worth of wages! This was a sum no one could ever repay.

So it is with our sin. God has forgiven us far more than we could ever repay. Because we have been forgiven much, He calls us to forgive others.

Lord,
You have forgiven us so much. Give us forgiving spirits so that – like You – we will forgive those who have offended us. In Jesus' name, Amen.

January 10

God's Image

"So God created man in His own image, in the image of God He created him; male and female He created them."

Genesis 1:27 (NIV)

If you ever travel to Vienna, Austria, try to visit Schönbrunn Palace, one of the most beautiful baroque palaces in Europe. Because Emperor Franz Joseph was born and raised there, many of his portraits hang on walls throughout the palace. If you look at these portraits, you won't actually see Franz Joseph, though. You'll only see an image of the popular emperor.

In a similar way, whenever we look at another person – another human being that God created – we see an image of God. Although God doesn't have a physical body, human beings are reflections of His glory, even though we are imperfect and finite. How amazing to think that God would choose to display His glory ... through us.

Father,
Help me to display Your glory in a way that's pleasing to You.
Amen.

Words

May the words of my mouth and the meditation
of my heart be pleasing to You, O Lord,
my rock and my redeemer.
Psalm 19:14

How many words do you think you speak a day? Research estimates that women generally speak about 15,000 words per day, while men speak about 7,000. Whether you speak more or less, that's still a lot of words.

When I consider the words of Psalm 19:14, I wonder ... of those thousands of words that I speak every day, how many of them are pleasing to God? Are they favorable? Gracious? Suitable? The words I speak are usually indications of what's going on in my heart. They are outward expressions of what I am thinking about. As I trust in the One who is my Rock and my Redeemer, my thoughts and words have the hope of being pleasing.

Lord,
May the words of my mouth and the thoughts of my heart please You. Amen.

January 12

The Eternal Kingdom

God will give you a grand entrance into the eternal
Kingdom of our Lord and Savior Jesus Christ.
2 Peter 1:11

On June 2 1953, the coronation of Her Majesty Queen Elizabeth II was held at Westminster Abbey. After her subjects paid their respects, the Archbishop prayed this prayer:

> God crown you with a crown of glory and righteousness,
> that having a right faith and manifold fruit of good works,
> you may obtain the crown of an everlasting kingdom
> by the gift of Him whose kingdom endureth forever. Amen.

No kingdom is everlasting save one: Jesus Christ's. The archbishop's prayer was an acknowledgment that as grand as human monarchs may be, they have merely a temporary reign. One day all of us will bow before the one and only King, to whom all reverence and honor is due.

> Sovereign Lord,
> May I be found faithful to You, so that on that day I will be prepared to shout, "You are worthy to receive all praise and glory and honor." Amen.

A Galloping Bridge

*He decided how hard the winds should blow
and how much rain should fall. He made the laws for
the rain and laid out a path for the lightning.*

Job 28:25-26

When the Tacoma Narrows Bridge opened for traffic in 1940, it was promptly nicknamed Galloping Gertie. Not only did the deck sway sideways, but it also moved up and down even in moderate winds. The movement was so severe that drivers reported vehicles ahead disappearing from their sight as they drove across. Four months after opening day, the bridge collapsed in a wind of only 42 miles per hour!

The disaster sparked a revolution in research to find out how winds affect bridges and design. God, the Creator already knew all that. In His wisdom, the Designer of the universe made all the laws that rule the physics of bridges and winds. God made everything and understands everything.

Creator God,
Thank You that there is nothing that You do not understand.
May we trust You with our lives today. Amen.

January 14

Enriching

*Who can find a virtuous and capable wife? She is more
precious than rubies. Her husband can trust her,
and she will greatly enrich his life. She brings him good,
not harm, all the days of her life.*

Proverbs 31:10-12

When I hear the word *enrich*, I tend to think of
vitamins and minerals that are added to food – or
investments that are added to a financial portfolio.
When we enrich something, we improve it, build it
up, or enhance it.

In God's good plan, He gives wives both the
privilege and the responsibility of enriching their
husbands' lives by building them up, supporting
them, and encouraging them. Proverbs 31:12 explains how we do this. Simply put, we must bring
our husbands good and not harm. Daily, we choose
to be an asset to them. We also choose not to under-
mine them or wound them. If you're married, think
of one way to enrich your husband today.

Father,
I want to bring my husband good, not harm. Guide me in this
endeavor. Amen.

January 15

Focus on God

Then [Jesus] said, "Beware! Guard against every kind of greed. Life is not measured by how much you own. Yes, a person is a fool to store up earthly wealth but not have a rich relationship with God."

Luke 12:15, 21

A man wanted Jesus' help and asked Him, "Please convince my brother to divide the family estate with me." Jesus – always coming from an eternal perspective – wanted the man to look upward. He warned the man not to become so horizontally focused on the things around him that he neglected to think vertically. There was something more important at stake – his relationship with God.

Sometimes we're like that man. In the middle of a crisis, we tend to focus on the problem and forget to look up. When we do look up to God, though, we experience His presence. And it is His presence that helps us put our questions and problems into proper perspective.

God,
May we look up to You and gain a healthy perspective. Amen.

January 16

Turning

*Turn us again to yourself, O Lord God
of Heaven's Armies. Make Your face shine
down upon us. Only then will we be saved.*
Psalm 80:19

Whether we're walking on a path or driving in a car, turning involves two distinct things. In order to turn toward something or someone, we are also turning away from something else. If I am turning right in order to head south, I'm turning away from going east.

Life is filled with many opportunities to turn – literally and figuratively. Based on where we're headed or what we're aiming at, each of us has choices to make – daily – about what we will turn toward and what we will turn from.

Only in turning to God can we realize His salvation and experience the light of His face shining on us. Only in turning to God can we turn away from things that would threaten to destroy us.

Lord God,
We turn to You for help and salvation. Please give us strength
to turn from things that would harm us. Amen.

Pursuing Love

Surely Your goodness and unfailing love will
pursue me all the days of my life, and I will live
in the house of the LORD forever.
Psalm 23:6

Have you ever been out for a walk and been followed by a dog? Hopefully, it was friendly!

The image of two (friendly) dogs chasing us might actually help us picture the way God's goodness and unfailing love follow us throughout our lives.

As you look back on your life so far, what are some of the ways in which God has pursued you? What people has He placed in your life to share the Good News with? How has He provided for you during times when you couldn't have made it through otherwise? Two friendly dogs might be able to maintain a chase for several hours, but God's goodness and unfailing love will last for much longer – they will chase us forever.

Father,
We are overwhelmed that You, Holy God, would pursue us.
Amen.

January 18

Prayer Makes a Difference

While Peter was in prison, the church
prayed very earnestly for him.
Acts 12:5

Overwhelmed. Gloomy. We would have felt that way, too, if we had been Peter's friends. After all, Jesus had been crucified at Passover the previous year, and James had just been killed by the sword. Peter seemed to be destined for the same end.

But Peter's friends were praying earnestly, and God sent an angel to lead him out of the prison – straight to a home where his friends were praying!

Are you aware of anyone who is praying for you today? Ask a family member or a friend to talk to God about your concerns. And if you're aware of someone who's in need of prayer, offer some passionate prayer to God on their behalf. Then, wait – because earnest prayer makes a difference.

Father,
Thank You that we can pray for one another. Amen.

January 19

Our Shepherd Provides

The Lord is my Shepherd; I have all that I need.
Psalm 23:1

New Zealand boasts more than 10 times as many sheep as people. The beautiful country is home to about 4 million people, and 47 million sheep!

Sheep are mentioned a lot in the Bible, providing fitting pictures of spiritual realities. Sheep are completely dependent on shepherds for food, water, guidance, and protection. Without a shepherd, sheep would never survive. But if a sheep is blessed to be under the care of a shepherd who leads it, protects it, and tends to its ailments; the sheep will live with a sense of security and serenity. With the Lord as our Shepherd, we can live that way, too. The Lord is my Shepherd; I have all that I need.

Lord and Shepherd,
We are needy people. Please guide us, protect us, and feed us through Your Word. Amen.

January 20

Expectant Prayers

*Listen to my voice in the morning, L*ORD*. Each morning
I bring my requests to You and wait expectantly.*
Psalm 5:3

Early morning is my favorite time of day. It's quiet
outside. It's quiet in the house. Instead of hearing
noise, traffic or voices, I hear the gentle sounds of
birds, rain, wind, or silence. That's what makes
morning such a good time for me to listen to God
through His Word and speak to Him in prayer.

As I read His Word, my mind is renewed. As I
wait expectantly for His response to my prayers,
I'm encouraged that others who lived before me –
like the psalmists – have experienced His answers,
too. As I see His provisions throughout each day,
I smile, thinking, "You heard my voice in the
morning, Lord!"

Loving Father,
Although You hear us anytime of the day or night, I'm especially grateful for the quiet of early morning. I want to pour out
my heart to You. Amen.

January 21

Hospitality Blesses

As [Lydia] listened to us, the Lord opened her heart ...
she asked us to be her guests. "If you agree that I am
a true believer in the Lord," she said, "come and stay at
my home." And she urged us until we agreed.

Acts 16:14-15

Perhaps you've enjoyed the hospitality of friends or family members who welcomed you into their hearts or homes with warmth and generosity. After receiving such hospitality, we often want to extend it to others. Hospitality has the potential to bless both the guest and the host. Guests have an opportunity to be refreshed, while hosts have occasion to see another person strengthened.

If someone has been hospitable to you, consider thanking them with a note, a phone call, or an e-mail. If you know someone who might be cheered by your hospitality, extend an invitation to them to come over for tea or take a walk together. It's a blessing to be a guest, but it's also a blessing to host a guest.

Father,
Because You have blessed us, may we extend that blessing to others. Amen.

Safe in His Hand

When the LORD spoke to Moses in the land of Egypt,
He said to him, "I am the LORD! Tell Pharaoh, the king
of Egypt, everything I am telling you." But Moses argued
with the LORD, saying, "I can't do it! I'm such a clumsy
speaker! Why should Pharaoh listen to me?"

Exodus 6:28-30

Moses is one of many characters in the Bible who intrigues me. Sometimes he argued with God. Sometimes he complained. Sometimes he questioned God. And what did God do? He listened. He cared. He asked Moses to pay close attention to Him, and He worked in powerful ways.

God does that with us too. We can bring our arguments, complaints and questions all to Him. Because God is the same now as He was in Moses' day, He will listen to us, care for us, ask us to pay close attention to Him, and work mightily. After Moses' questions, where did he land? "So Moses did just as the LORD had commanded" (Exod. 7:6). Hopefully, we will too.

God,
We are incredibly grateful for Your patience with us. May we follow You closely. Amen.

January 23

Walls of Safety

So on October 2 the wall was finished – just fifty-two days after we had begun … this work had been done with the help of our God.
Nehemiah 6:15-16

Walls were such a common part of ancient life that a city without one was unimaginable. Walls provided strength, protection, and even beauty. Though people left the city to farm, travel, or trade, it was to their home within the walls that they returned. Nehemiah was understandably distressed to learn that Jerusalem's wall had been torn down, so it was a day of great joy when the reconstructed wall was completed. Nehemiah understood the essential role walls played in the life of Israel.

In the Bible, walls depict the safety we can find in God, as well as the dreadful results we experience when we operate outside of His protected plan. Living within the "walls" of God's protective care offers us security, not confinement.

January 24

Lord,
Sometimes we look over the walls of Your care, thinking that things on the other side are more green and lush. Help us to find joy and security in the confines of Your care. Amen.

Magnificent Power

Have you entered the storehouses of the snow or seen the
storehouses of the hail? Do you know the laws of the
heavens? Can you set up God's dominion over the earth?
Job 38:22, 33 (NIV)

If you lived in Cervinia, Italy, falling snow would be
no unusual occurrence. The ski resort town receives
about 400 inches of snow each year. For people who
lived in Bible times, however, snow was not com-
monplace. It fell only once every several years. It's
interesting, then, that when God spoke to Job from
a whirlwind, He used the image of snow to point to
the reality of His mystery and power.

Where have you seen snow? Whether you've
seen it in Italy, Switzerland, or Colorado, you've
witnessed something straight from God's storehouses, something that is evidence of His magnificent power. God, who has the power to send snow,
has the power to help us, too.

Father,
Thank You for beautiful glimpses of Your power. Amen.

January 25

Pour Out Your Heart

O my people, trust in Him at all times.
Pour out your heart to Him, for God is our refuge.
Psalm 62:8

If you order a milkshake at Stella's in West Des Moines, the waiter or waitress will ask if you'd like to lie down on your back! If you agree, he or she will give you an empty glass to hold (upright) on your forehead. The waiter or waitress will then proceed to pour a milkshake into the glass while you're lying down and he or she is standing! The challenge is to pour the contents into the glass without spilling. Pouring is sometimes a messy endeavor.

Pouring out our hearts can be messy, too. When we begin talking to God about what's in our hearts, the contents might surprise us and the gush might feel a bit messy. I doubt that God cares much about the mess, though. He came to earth to help us deal with our messes. So, just start pouring.

Father,
May we realize that the feelings and contents of our hearts are completely safe with You. You already know it all. Amen.

January 26

Fear?

Fear of the LORD is the foundation of true wisdom.
All who obey His commandments will grow in widsom.
Psalm 111:10

Do you want to understand what is true, right, and lasting? Would you like to grow in insight, common sense, and discernment? You won't need money to acquire it, but you will need fear. Not the kind of fear that's caused by a sense of danger, but the kind of fear that generates extreme awe, reverence, and respect for God. That's the foundation of wisdom.

Foundations are set in place to be built on, and this foundation is no different. As we honor God, live in awe of His power, and obey His Word, wisdom will develop in every area of our lives. Do you want to be wise? Grow in fear and awe of God!

Father,
We need Your wisdom daily. May we spend time in Your Word and increase our awe of You. Amen.

Give Your Cares to God

*Give all your worries and cares to God,
for He cares about you.*
1 Peter 5:7

If you decide to give your friend a book, you might hand it to her, drop it off at her house, or leave it in her car. However you choose to do it, you are the one who gives up the book and your friend is the one who receives it.

The process of giving our worries and cares to God is similar – it's active, not passive, and involves a giver and a receiver. One obvious benefit in giving God our worries and cares is that we're able to get rid of troublesome thoughts. A second benefit is that we're giving our concerns to someone who cares about us.

Perhaps the greatest benefit to giving our worries and cares to God is this: because He is all-loving, all-wise, and all-powerful, He can help us better than anyone else!

Father,
We tend to hang onto our cares and worry about them. We want to bring them to You instead. Amen.

January 28

Wordless Message

The heavens proclaim the glory of God. The skies
display His craftsmanship. Day after day they continue
to speak; night after night they make Him known.
They speak without a sound or a word; their voice
is never heard. Yet their message has gone throughout
the earth, and their words to all the world.

Psalm 19:1-4

Every day we convey messages to one another without using any words. We smile; we scowl; we hum quietly; we tap our fingers. God conveys messages without words, too. Have you ever walked outside on a clear night, seen the brilliance of the full moon, and thought, *That is spectacular!*

You were responding to God's wordless message that's available to the whole world – the message of His glory. As Isaac Watts wrote, "Nature with open volume stands to spread her Maker's praise abroad." Year after year, night after night, looking up into the heavensreminds us of God's power and love – without Him having to say a single word.

Father,
Thank You for spreading Your glory across the night sky for us to see. Amen.

January 29

White As Snow

*"Come now, let's settle this," says the LORD.
"Though your sins are like scarlet, I will make them
as white as snow. Though they are red like crimson,
I will make them as white as wool."*

Isaiah 1:18

As I gaze out my window this frosty morning, everything is covered with a blanket of freshly fallen snow. Once the snowplows appear, the scene will start to get a little dirty, but for now it looks clean.

Freshly fallen snow is an image of what our dark hearts look like after we have been forgiven by God. When Jesus shed His blood on the cross for my sins and yours, He made it possible for our hearts to be cleansed bright white. When we confess our sin to God and ask for His forgiveness, He graciously makes our hearts as white as snow. *What can wash away my sin? Nothing – but the blood of Jesus!*

Father,
For clean hearts that Jesus' blood makes possible, we thank You. Amen.

Look Up

*Patient endurance is what you need now,
so that you will continue to do God's will. Then you
will receive all that He has promised. "For in just a little
while, the Coming One will come and not delay.
And my righteous ones will live by faith."*

Hebrews 10:36-38

When driving on major expressways, it's not uncommon for us to come upon signs that flash the message: EXPECT DELAYS. Delays keep us sitting in traffic and sometimes leave us feeling frustrated because our plans for the day have been hindered.

Other times we experience interruptions in life that present us with larger delays like illness, job loss, or broken relationships. Although these situations might tempt us to blow up or give up, a good choice is to *look* up. Because God has helped others in the past, we can be confident that He is willing to help us too. Righteous people live by faith. Righteous people look up.

Father,
When we feel like giving up, please give us Your strength to endure. We want to look up! Amen.

January 31

February

Knowing God

"Be still, and know that I am God! I will be honored by every nation. I will be honored throughout the world."

Psalm 46:10

Have you ever known a person who later went on to become very famous? Perhaps it was a childhood friend of yours who grew up and won a gold medal in the Olympics. Maybe a person you served with on a committee was chosen by the President of the United States to become a member of his cabinet. Now, you say, "I knew him or her when ..."

Someday, every person from every nation in the world will bend their knee to Christ and confess allegiance to His name. At that time, those of us who are spending time with Him now will be grateful that we got to know Him while we were here on earth. Ultimately, God will be honored by everyone.

Father,
Thank You that knowing You here on earth prepares us for honoring You forever in heaven. Amen.

February 1

Three Kings' Favor

*Praise the LORD, the God of our ancestors, who made
the king want to beautify the Temple of the LORD
in Jerusalem! I felt encouraged because the
gracious hand of the LORD my God was on me.*
Ezra 7:27-28

The Old Testament book of Ezra is a remarkable history of how God favored His people before their enemies. The Israelites had been exiled from the Promised Land because of their sin, but God stirred the hearts of three pagan kings to restore them to their homeland. They issued decrees directing Jewish people to return and rebuild the city of Jerusalem and its Temple. King Artaxerxes even ordered that they be given great wealth, 24 tons of silver, 7,500 pounds of silver articles, and 7,500 pounds of gold!

Why would the empire sanction such a raid on the treasury? Only because the gracious hand of God had stirred his heart!

Lord,
There are times when the circumstances of life seem insurmountable. Thank You that in Your grace, You move people and circumstances to accomplish Your will. Amen.

February 2

Move toward Holiness

Stay away from every kind of evil. Now may the God of peace make you holy in every way, and may your whole spirit and soul and body be kept blameless until our Lord Jesus Christ comes again. God will make this happen, for He who calls you is faithful.

1 Thessalonians 5:22-23

Only God can make us holy. It's our responsibility, however, to make choices that move us in that direction. If I told you that I wanted to travel north, but immediately headed south, I'd be sabotaging my goal. If I told you that I wanted to be holy, but pursued evil, I'd be undermining my goal. The apostle Paul spoke to the believers in Thessalonica about this very issue.

He encouraged them to move in the direction of holiness, avoiding evil, and God would be faithful to make them holy. Holiness is a process that begins and continues with God, but it's our responsibility not to sabotage the process.

Father,
Thank You for the freedom to make choices. We want to choose things that help us grow in holiness. Amen.

February 3

A Good Reputation

*A good reputation is more
valuable than costly perfume.*
Ecclesiastes 7:1

The Comoros islands, off the southeast coast of Africa, export about 80% of the world's supply of *ylang ylang* – the main ingredient of expensive perfumes like Chanel No. 5. Costly by most country's standards, *ylang ylang* is sold from the Comoros at the price of about CFr 23,000 per kilogram – in USD that's about $116 per pound.

Refreshing as the essence of any expensive perfume is, the Bible reminds us that a good reputation is of much greater value. Just as high-class perfumes are made from costly ingredients, good reputations are made from godly attitudes, words, and actions. Thankfully, we're not left to produce these on our own. God's Word and Spirit are His guiding resources.

Father,
May we never underestimate the value of a good reputation.
Amen.

February 4

Light in Darkness

I could ask the darkness to hide me and the light around me to become night – but even in darkness I cannot hide from You. To You the night shines as bright as day. Darkness and light are the same to You.

Psalm 139:11-12

As a child, I was terrified of the dark. Many nights, I chose to sleep with my closet light on. Although I don't sleep with the closet light on anymore, I still don't like the absence of light. My husband knows that if he turns off the lights in our basement while I'm down there doing laundry, I'll scream!

Years ago, I found immense comfort in realizing that, to God, the night shines as bright as day. The Bible assures me that God is Light and there is no darkness in Him (1 John 1:5). So whether I'm in the light or in the dark, it's all the same to Him. It's comforting to know that I can never be lost to God.

God of Light,
Thank You that I can find security in Your Light. Amen.

February 5

Abba Father

*So you have not received a spirit that makes
you fearful slaves. Instead, you received God's Spirit
when He adopted you as His own children.
Now we call Him, "Abba, Father." For His Spirit joins
with our spirit to affirm that we are God's children.*
Romans 8:15-16

According to research done by Dr. Davis and Dr. MacNeilage at the University of Texas, baby-babbling patterns are common among many languages around the world. Davis says, "One of the hallmarks of typical baby babble is rhythmicity, meaning all the syllables are about the same length. An example would be repeating 'ba-ba-ba-ba.'"

Paul's use of the word has its origin in the Aramaic word *ab-bah*, a curious similarity consistent with the researcher's findings. Anyone who has observed an infant knows the joy a father has when his child babbles the words *Ba-ba* or *Da-Da*! We are God's children and He is longing to hear us say *Ab-ba*.

Abba Father,
Thank You that I am Your child, and that You take great joy in hearing my prayers. Amen.

February 6

The "Who" Question

*"I have heard all about You, LORD. I am filled
with awe by Your amazing works. In this time of our
deep need, help us again as You did in years gone by.
And in Your anger, remember Your mercy."*
Habakkuk 3:2

The question "Why?" is frequently heard from the
lips of three-year-olds, but adults ask it too. When
we don't understand events going on around us,
we wonder "Why?" When things seem unfair, we
inquire "Why?"

The Old Testament prophet Habakkuk boldly
asked God the same questions – and more. Surprisingly, God didn't answer the "Why?" question – He
answered the "Who?" question instead. Habakkuk
was encouraged to trust that God is full of power,
love, and justice, and that He is in control.

Asking the "Who?" question helps us to no longer despair but to grow in confidence. The 'answer'
to that query is found in a trusting relationship with
the one and only God.

Father,
Thank You that focusing on You instead of "Why?" helps us to
gain proper perspective. Amen.

February 7

Longing for Water

As the deer longs for streams of water, so I long for You,
O God. I thirst for God, the living God.
When can I go and stand before Him?

Psalm 42:1-2

You don't have to teach a deer to look for water. Anyone who has watched a nature show on television has seen the way animals congregate at watering holes to satisfy their thirst. God has built that thirst into animals' natures and they gravitate toward water to quench it.

People have the same thirst. From the first moments of life, infants instinctively suck, in search of their mother's milk. The psalmist sees what the human heart is like – thirsty for God.

Some people attempt to satisfy their thirst through things that can never quench it. Those who are wise and discerning recognize that God has made us for Himself, and it is only in Him that we are able to find true satisfaction.

Lord,
Help me to recognize my desire as a longing for You. May I be quick to come to You for satisfaction. Amen.

Faithful Hospitality

*Dear friend, you are being faithful to God
when you care for the traveling teachers who
pass through, even though they are strangers to you.*
3 John 1:5

Elegant meals, fine china, and fancy centerpieces –
hospitality may include these things, but it extends
way beyond large gatherings and small dinner
parties. Hospitality is mostly about showing care
to others, demonstrating a personal concern and
interest for what's going on in their lives.

Sometimes people need a place to stay, and you
have a room available. Other times a friend who is
hospitalized needs a cheerful visit. Perhaps your
neighbor is a widow who has no one to check in
on her when she's ill. Asking yourself the question,
"How might I bring warmth and cheer to this
person?" is a good place to begin.

Father,
May I be faithful to You by showing hospitality to others.
Amen.

Wait Quietly

*I wait quietly before God, for my victory comes
from Him. Let all that I am wait quietly before God,
for my hope is in Him. He alone is my rock and
my salvation, my fortress where I will not be shaken.*

Psalm 62:1, 5

Several hours after my family boarded an airplane in Munich, we were informed that our
10-hour flight to Chicago had been canceled. After
waiting in line – again – for several more hours, we
made a delightful discovery.

The airline had arranged for us to stay at a fancy hotel, with a complimentary gourmet dinner
and breakfast. On top of that, they issued us first-
class seats on the next day's flight from Munich to
Chicago! I felt excited – and chagrined. I had been
waiting impatiently, when there was a gift right
around the corner.

Heaven is right around the corner too. We can
wait patiently by trusting Christ and remembering
that God is in control.

God,
In our times of waiting, please bring Your peace and quiet to
our hearts. Amen.

Lasting Priorities

You have planted much but harvest little. You eat but are not satisfied. You drink but are still thirsty. You put on clothes but cannot keep warm. Your wages disappear as though you were putting them in pockets filled with holes!

Haggai 1:6

Twenty-five hundred years ago, the prophet Haggai challenged the Jewish people to re-evaluate their priorities because something was out of balance. While the Jewish people were living in luxurious houses, God's house was lying in ruins. Haggai helped the people to see that even though they were busy rushing from one seemingly good thing to the next, they weren't focusing on what was most important and they weren't accomplishing anything lasting.

It's easy for us to do that, too. What God desires from us today is the same thing He desired from the Jewish people so many years ago. He wants what is important to Him – His kingdom – to become important to us. That's what will last.

Father,
Sometimes we're so busy, but unproductive. Please give us Your wisdom to focus on what is eternal. Amen.

February 11

Encourage the Timid

Encourage those who are timid.
1 Thessalonians 5:14

Do you live with, work with, or know anyone who is timid? Timid people are often modest, shy, or easily intimidated, and it doesn't take much to alarm them, demoralize them, or threaten them. That's where encouragement comes in.

The next time you encounter a timid person, think of it as an opportunity to be encouraging. How can you express your interest in them? What can you say that might be a boost to them? Is there a way that you might help to relieve this person's anxiety?

By serving, reassuring, or smiling, you have an opportunity to be one of God's messengers. Even just a little encouragement goes a long way.

Father,
May we be encouraging to people around us who are feeling intimidated. Amen.

February 12

Recall God's Faithfulness

Go, inspect the city of Jerusalem ... the many towers ... the fortified walls ... the citadels, that you may describe them to future generations. For that is what God is like. He is our God forever and ever, and He will guide us until we die.
Psalm 48:12-14

It's good to recall times in our lives when God helped, protected, or rescued us. Passing those stories on to our children, grandchildren, nieces or nephews is even better. In Psalm 48, a foreign army was about to attack the gates of Jerusalem, but God miraculously threw the enemy into a panic. Because the people of Jerusalem were protected, they went on a 'post-victory' tour of the city, and praised God for His help and intervention in their lives. This became a wonderful story to share with future generations.

How has God helped and guided you? Consider how you might share His faithfulness to a younger member of your family.

Father,
We want to recall Your faithfulness to future generations so that Your glory may be remembered always. Amen.

February 13

Promises Kept

"The mountains may move and the hills disappear,
but even then My faithful love for you will remain.
My covenant of blessing will never be broken,"
says the LORD, who has mercy on you.

Isaiah 54:10

When you hear the phrase 'moving a mountain,' what comes to mind? Losing 20 pounds? Cleaning out your garage? The world's race to deal with AIDS? To liken something to 'moving a mountain' means it is incredibly difficult, if not flat-out impossible, to do.

In order for physical mountains to move, plates underneath the surface of the earth would need to shift, volcanoes would need to erupt, or earthquakes would need to occur.

Thankfully, none of these are everyday happenings. God used the picture of mountains moving to assure us that even if the unlikely should ever happen, His faithful love will always remain and His promises will never be broken.

Father,
For the promise of Your love, we thank You. Amen.

February 14

An Amazing Stretch

"I am the one who made the earth and created people
to live on it. With My hands I stretched out the heavens.
All the stars are at My command."
Isaiah 45:12

Do you know how long your arm span is? Usually, it's about the same measurement as your height. With that distance in mind, what kinds of things could you stretch out with your hands? A luggage strap, five feet of ribbon, a dog's leash?

The difference between what we can stretch out with our hands and what God can stretch out with His – the heavens – is so vast that we can hardly imagine it. When we ponder how distinctly *other* God is from us, we want to thank Him that He – the Lord of the universe – was willing to come into our world so that we could have a relationship with Him. That was an amazing stretch.

Father God,
Thank You that You created us and that You want to have a relationship with us. Amen.

Refreshing Rest

"Come to Me, all of you who are weary and carry heavy burdens, and I will give you rest. Take My yoke upon you. Let Me teach you, because I am humble and gentle at heart, and you will find rest for your souls. For My yoke is easy to bear, and the burden I give you is light."

Matthew 11:28-30

Many world religions involve a lot of rules and regulations. Do this ... Don't do that ... The first challenge is to learn the rules, but an even bigger challenge is to follow them. In such religions, the degree to which people carry out the rules and regulations usually defines the quality of their existence – often tense and insecure.

In the Bible, God shows us the pathway to life, but He doesn't expect us to walk it on our own. He actually offers to come and live inside us. Instead of weighing us down with impossible demands, He offers us rest in Him as we depend on what Christ has already accomplished for us on the cross.

Father,
Thank You for sending Jesus to do the agonizing work of salvation so that our souls can find rest in You. Amen.

February 16

Confidence in God

Don't put your trust in mere humans.
They are as frail as breath.
Isaiah 2:22
Blessed are those who trust in the LORD and have
made the LORD their hope and confidence.
Jeremiah 17:7

How much air can one breath provide? Enough for us to gulp down a few sips of water. How long does one breath last? That depends. For most of us, a breath lasts just a few seconds. For a freediver with huge pulmonary capacity and lots of training, it might be a few minutes. Either way, one breath doesn't last very long.

The Bible cautions us not to put our trust in human beings, because humans are as frail as breath. Instead, we're encouraged to trust in God. If you're facing challenges today that seem overwhelming, express your feelings to God and ask Him for His help. That's one step toward making Him your hope and confidence. As you depend on Him, you will be blessed.

Father,
You are worthy of our confidence and trust. Amen.

Undeserved Kindness

When God our Savior revealed His kindness and love,
He saved us, not because of the righteous things we had done,
but because of His mercy. He washed away our sins, giving
us a new birth and new life through the Holy Spirit.

Titus 3:4-6

Some years ago, my husband and I learned of a refugee couple who had just moved to our town. We wanted to help them so we began by introducing them to people at our church. Over time, our church community was able to provide the couple with a job, an apartment, and enough clothing, furniture, and household supplies to begin their lives here. Our gifts to the young family were not based on anything they did to earn them. They were simply gifts of mercy and kindness.

Spiritually speaking, all of us are like refugees. We have nothing to offer God and yet He loves us and wants to provide for us. He forgives our sins and gives us new life through the Holy Spirit. All because of His great mercy.

Father,
We're grateful for Your mercy because we know we've done nothing to deserve it. Amen.

February 18

God Reveals His Thoughts

The LORD is the one who shaped the mountains, stirs up the winds, and reveals His thoughts to mankind. He turns the light of dawn into darkness and treads on the heights of the earth. The LORD God of Heaven's Armies is His name!

Amos 4:13

How do you *shape* a mountain, anyway? By creating it, forming it, and sculpting it, for starters. Located in Asia and standing 29,035 ft (8,850 m) tall, Mount Everest is one of the most famous mountains that God shaped. Mathematical documentation, proving Mount Everest to be the tallest summit in the world, didn't become available until 1852, although God has known it all along.

Something else He has known all along and has been making known to us since Creation is His thoughts. When we seek a relationship with God through faith in Christ, God's Spirit comes to live in our hearts and share His thoughts with us (1 Cor. 2:11-12). The God who shaped Mount Everest is willing to share His thoughts with us!

Lord God of Heaven's Armies,
May we be quiet enough before You to hear Your thoughts.
Amen.

February 19

Never Separated

I am convinced that nothing can ever separate us from God's love. Neither death nor life, neither angels nor demons, neither our fears for today nor our worries about tomorrow – not even the powers of hell can separate us from God's love.

Romans 8:38

Most of us have felt the pain of being separated from someone close to us. Maybe a friend moved away or stopped calling. Perhaps a family member or friend left his or her community to serve in the military on the other side of the world. Some of us might have been rejected or abandoned by parents or a spouse.

Whether we try to ignore it, minimize it, medicate it, or grieve it; separation hurts. Separation is a part of life. Since all of us feel the pain of it at one time or another, it's comforting to read that there is nothing – NOTHING – that can ever separate us from Christ's love.

Father,
Thank You that because Your Son, Jesus, was once separated from You on the cross, we can be confident that we will not be.
Amen.

February 20

Power Belongs to God

*God has spoken plainly, and I have heard
it many times; Power, O God, belongs to You;
unfailing love, O Lord, is Yours.*
Psalm 62:11-12

Sometimes we feel weak and intimidated. We observe another person's abilities, competence, or influence and it gives us cause for pause. At times like that, it's easy for our perspective to become skewed and distorted, thinking that power is found in wealth, education, or talent. Clearly, it's not. In the exact words of the Bible, "God has spoken plainly ... Power, O God, belongs to You." God doesn't need our strength. He wants us to wait for Him, to trust Him, to pour out our hearts to Him, and to accept His love.

When we rest in the security of His love for us, we're prompted to serve Him out of grateful hearts with the power that He provides. Power belongs to God.

Father,
We are totally dependent on Your strength. Amen.

Treasure Field

*"The Kingdom of Heaven is like a treasure that
a man discovered hidden in a field.
In his excitement, he hid it again and sold everything
he owned to get enough money to buy the field."*
Matthew 13:44

The headline read, "Texas couple finds 6.35-carat diamond today at Arkansas's Crater of Diamonds State Park." Located in Murfreesboro, Arkansas, the park contains the only diamond mine in the world that is open to the public. Each year more than 600 diamonds are found by visitors. The crater itself is a 35-acre field that is plowed to bring the gemstones to the surface.

When Jesus told the story of the treasure hidden in the field, He emphasized both the extreme value of the treasure and the joy of those who find it. When we discover the incredible riches of Christ and the inheritance He offers us, we're willing to make sacrifices in order to claim our treasure.

Lord,
Give me vision to see all You have offered me as a free gift. Help me to find great joy in the treasure of who You are. Amen.

February 22

God's Crown Jewels

On that day the LORD their God will rescue His people.
They will sparkle in His land like jewels in a crown.
How wonderful and beautiful they will be!
Zechariah 9:16-17

Kept under highest security, the Crown Jewels of England are displayed at the Tower of London. The Imperial State Crown, made of gold in 1937 for King George VI, includes 2,868 diamonds, 273 pearls, 17 sapphires, 11 emeralds, and 5 rubies. While such treasure is nearly impossible for most of us to fathom, it does give us a clue as to how much God values us.

Zechariah said that the Lord's people will "sparkle in His land like jewels in a crown." What is the source of our beauty? Like diamonds, we have no inherent light source. But our beauty can be seen as we reflect the magnificent glory of God!

Lord,
Help me live my life to reflect the spectacular light of Your glory.
May those around me recognize the many facets of who You are. Amen.

February 23

Water As Still As Glass

*"I am leaving you with a gift – peace of mind and heart.
And the peace I give is a gift the world cannot give.
So don't be troubled or afraid."*

John 14:27

The water was still as glass. As the sky began to lighten, the peaceful water reflected scattered clouds and tall buildings. Early morning on Florida's inter-coastal waterway begins with an almost surrealistic silence and peace. It was quite a contrast from the previous day, when a parade of boats churned up the water for hour after hour.

Our hearts are not unlike that water – sometimes churned up by circumstances we face our fears we haven't faced. Jesus promised us a gift – peace of mind and heart. Embracing that peace sometimes requires rest, a time of prayer, or the wise counsel of a friend. Always, the peace comes from Jesus Himself who is our peace.

Lord Jesus,
Thank You that You offer me the gift of peace. May I be ready and willing to turn all my cares over to You this day. Amen.

God Formed Us

"I knew you before I formed you in your mother's womb. Before you were born I set you apart and appointed you as My prophet to the nations."
Jeremiah 1:5

For days when we feel inadequate, it's helpful to refer to words that God spoke through the prophet Jeremiah. God formed us. He created us, brought us into existence, and put us together. Before He formed us, He knew us. Our husbands, parents, or friends may not always understand us, but God does.

God set us apart. He wants us to love Him, obey Him, and serve Him. He appointed things for each of us to do for His Kingdom. If we haven't discovered them yet, we can ask Him! He's delighted when we want to do His will. God knows us and has good plans for us.

Father,
Thank You for Your Word that encourages us when we are feeling discouraged. Amen.

February 25

God's Gifts

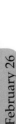

I remember your genuine faith. This is why I remind you to fan into flames the spiritual gift God gave you ... For God has not given us a spirit of fear and timidity, but of power, love, and self-discipline.

2 Timothy 1:5-7

A person who struggles with aggression might have difficulty understanding a person who battles with timidity. But those who tend to be apprehensive, unassertive or easily intimidated would understand completely. Timothy struggled with timidity. It's interesting that Paul's message to Timothy was not, "Come on, Timothy, you can do it. You've just got to believe in yourself!" Paul urged him to focus on what God's Spirit could do in and through him.

How would Timothy find help with power, love, and self-discipline? Through faith. Through Timothy's faith in Christ, God's Spirit would provide. God is the giver of gifts, and through the power of His Spirit, He equips us to use them.

Father,
May we acknowledge, value, and use the gifts You have given to us. Amen.

February 26

Old Faithful

The faithful love of the LORD never ends!
His mercies never cease. Great is His faithfulness;
His mercies begin afresh each morning.
Lamentations 3:22-23

Perhaps the most famous attraction at Yellowstone National Park is a geyser that erupts about every 91 minutes, spewing up to 8,400 gallons (32,000 liters) of scalding water to a height of 180 ft. (55 m). It's called "Old Faithful."

The people of Israel needed a vision of something faithful while they were in exile in Babylon. Having been carried off because of their sins and forced to settle in a place far from home, they felt that all was lost. Deep grief hung over them as they contemplated the violent destruction of their homes and their glorious temple. It was in this setting that Jeremiah wrote the lofty lines of comfort found in Lamentations. In the midst of suffering and loss, He assured them that the faithful love and mercy of the Lord never ends!

Lord,
Help us to remember that in all things, at all times, You are faithful. In Jesus' name, Amen.

February 27

First and Last

"I, Jesus, have sent My angel to give you this message for the churches. I am both the source of David and the heir to his throne. I am the bright morning star."
Revelation 22:16

Many people who come upon genealogies in the Bible react with boredom. Sometimes we even skip over them and move on to another passage. From Genesis to Revelation, the Bible includes so many genealogies that we're wise to take heed. There are some interesting things to discover in them.

In Revelation 22, the very last chapter of the Bible, Jesus gives John perhaps the shortest, most encompassing genealogical summary ever. He says He is both the source and heir of David! How is it possible to be contained at both the beginning and the ending of a royal line? It is possible only if one were both eternally God and actually human. Thus, Jesus rightfully claims to be the Source, Ancestor, and Heir to the throne of King David.

Lord Jesus,
Thank You that You are the First and the Last, the Alpha and Omega. May I live in wonder and obedience under Your eternal care. Amen.

March

God Loves Humility

*The high and lofty one who lives in eternity,
the Holy One, says this: "I live in the high and holy place
with those whose spirits are contrite and humble.
I restore the crushed spirit of the humble and revive the courage of those with repentant hearts."*

Isaiah 57:15

Have you noticed that many people who are powerful and prominent tend to spend time with other people who are equally as distinguished or influential? God is not like that. He approaches relationships in a much different way. God – the Creator and King of all the earth – declares that He lives with those whose spirits are repentant and unassuming. God, who lives in a high and lofty place, comes down to us, because there's nothing we could ever do to lift ourselves up to Him.

When we humble ourselves before Him and live in repentance He elevates us, refreshes us, and gives us new courage. Now there's a lift for a sagging spirit!

Gracious Father,
We're grateful that You – Holy God – are willing to inhabit our repentant hearts. Thank You for reviving us. Amen.

March 1

Extreme Swallow

"You strain your water so you won't accidentally swallow a gnat, but you swallow a camel!"
Matthew 23:24

My local newspaper recently reported that a 12-foot Burmese Python snake swallowed an entire queen-sized electric blanket – including the electrical cord and control box! That was one extreme swallow. The snake's owner was grateful that after a two-hour surgery, the blanket was successfully removed from the 60-pound reptile.

During New Testament times, the Pharisees sometimes strained their water in order to avoid swallowing unclean insects. But – Jesus pointed out – some of them would turn around and "swallow a camel". What might "swallowing a camel" look like for us? Perhaps it's tithing 15% of an income, but cheating on taxes. Maybe it's protecting a person physically, but killing them emotionally. It's wise for each of us to think about what we are straining and what we are swallowing.

March 2

Father,
Please give us wisdom to see things from Your perspective.
Amen.

Return to God

Return to the LORD your God, for He is merciful and compassionate, slow to get angry and filled with unfailing love. He is eager to relent and not punish.

Joel 2:13

There's a tea shop in Harrogate, England that I'd like to return to someday because they had scrumptious tea and scones. Have you ever spent time away from a person or place that you especially liked, and thought it would be pleasant to return – pleasant to come back?

Sometimes we realize that – for whatever reason – we've been away from God and we want to come back to Him. How gracious God is to accept us back after times when we have left His path and wandered off in search of other things. When we return to God, we come back to mercy, compassion, and unfailing love. Nowhere else will we find such healing and hope.

Gracious Father,
Thank You that even when we have moved away from You,
You are eager for us to return. Amen.

March 3

Deal with Hatred

*Do not nurse hatred in your heart for any of your
relatives. Confront people directly so you will not
be held guilty for their sin.* Leviticus 19:17
Hiding hatred makes you a liar. Proverbs 10:18
*Love must be sincere. Hate what is evil;
cling to what is good.* Romans 12:9 (NIV)

Sometimes I walk alongside friends who struggle
with hatred of one sort or another. Feeling hatred
toward someone who hurt us isn't surprising – the
Psalms tell us that even God is angry with the wicked. Letting hatred take over, though, is unhealthy.

People who are honest about hatred, process it
with wise friends or counselors, ask God for help,
and speak the truth in love to those around them,
make huge strides. Those who aren't honest about
their hatred, and try to conceal or suppress it, frequently have bigger problems later.

God offers us helpful tools to deal with hatred –
are we using them?

Father,
We are grateful that You understand our feelings. Please help
us to deal with them constructively. Amen.

March 4

A Promised Visit

*Praise the Lord, the God of Israel, because He has visited
and redeemed His people. He has sent us a mighty Savior
from the royal line of His servant David, just as He
promised through His holy prophets long ago.*
Luke 1:68-70

Years ago, when my young son, Jordan, had surgery to repair a broken femur, approximately fifty
people visited him over the course of about a week.
As a result of those visits, our whole family felt
warmed. The message conveyed by the visits was
that people cared about our family, about us.

When God sent Jesus to be born on this earth
over two thousand years ago, that's the message He
gave to us. God sent Jesus to pay much more than
a friendly visit, though. Jesus' visit paid for our
sins, and His sojourn on earth included death on a
cross. The message He gave to us was – and still is –
"I care about you enough to die for you."

Father,
Jesus' visit to earth to die for our sins made it possible for You to
live in our hearts. We are forever grateful. Amen.

March 5

Hiding Place

*For You are my hiding place; You protect me
from trouble. You surround me with songs of victory.*

Psalm 32:7

What does *hiding* prompt you to think of? Hide-and-seek when you were a child? Covering up some of your insecurities as an adult? It's curious to me that God is described in the Bible as our hiding place. The One who made us and knows everything about us, the One who is full of perfect justice and knows exactly what each of us really deserves, wants us to hide ourselves in Him.

God, the only One in the world who is perfect, is not against us. He is for us. In fact, He is more for us than anyone else has ever been or will be. Today, at moments when you might feel the urge to hide, run to God. He surrounds those who trust Him with unfailing love. He is the safest hiding place in the world.

Father,
We are grateful that we don't need to hide from You — the One who knows everything about us. Amen.

March 6

Longing for Justice

Your righteousness is like the mighty mountains,
Your justice like the ocean depths.

Psalm 36:6

Those of you who have snorkeled know that the instant you open your eyes under the surface of the ocean, you feel as though you've entered a whole new world.

Some parts of the world extend much deeper than we might think. The Hjort Trench in Australia measures about 6,000 meters under the surface of the water. That's deep enough to fit more than two of Australia's highest mountains stacked on top of each other!

When the Bible tells us that God's justice is similar to the ocean depths, we get the picture. It is unfathomable or immeasurable. Next time you feel a longing for justice – whether for yourself or on behalf of another – appeal to the One whose justice is like the depths of the ocean.

God,
When we long to understand or experience justice in a particular situation, may we run to You, because You are full of justice. Amen.

March 7

Love Begins with God

*No one has ever seen God. But if we love
each other, God lives in us, and His
love is brought to full expression in us.*
1 John 4:12

When a Christian shows love to another Christian, God is revealed to a watching world. Whether it's offering your home to a weekend guest who needs a place to stay, or visiting a friend in the hospital, one Christian showing love to another Christian is one of the ways we see God's love in action.

That's not too difficult when things are going well, but what about the times when loving another person feels challenging, if not downright impossible? It's good to remember that love did not begin with us. Since God is both the origin and the source of love, we can run to Him when our well of love seems to have run dry. We can always draw more from Him.

God,
Please help us to treat our brothers and sisters in Christ with love. Even though You are invisible, this is how You can be seen in us! Amen.

March 8

God's Voice Thunders

*My heart pounds as I think of this. It trembles
within me. Listen carefully to the thunder
of God's voice as it rolls from His mouth.
It rolls across the heavens, and His lightning flashes
in every direction. God's voice is glorious in the thunder.*

Job 37:1-3, 5

My husband's flight was climbing into a turbulent sky as it departed for Seattle, Washington. The winds buffeted the plane and suddenly there was a huge explosion and a flash of light. Jim's first thought was that the engine had exploded and that he would be late for his meeting. His second thought was that he might not make it at all! But the plane had only been struck by lightning, and all was well.

Sometimes, we go through our days oblivious to what God may be trying to say to us. Occasionally, God's voice explodes into our lives, speaking in such a dramatic way that our hearts leap within us. In those times, it is good for us to listen carefully to what He is saying.

Lord,
May we listen alertly to You and respond to Your voice. Amen.

March 9

Bright Lights

Live clean, innocent lives as children of God, shining like bright lights in a world full of crooked and perverse people.
Philippians 2:15

In March of 2000, one of the grandest displays of the Northern Lights was observed from Finland. Excited people roused their neighbors in the middle of the night. "Don't waste any time," they said. "Go outside and look at the dazzling sky – you won't believe your eyes!" Also known as Aurora Borealis, the spectacular blaze of colored light appeared in the northern sky. Scientists tell us this blaze of light occurs when material that's thrown off the sun's surface collides with the earth's atmosphere.

"Bright light in the world" is what the apostle Paul used to describe what a clean and innocent life looks like in a world full of darkness. When we live righteously, we can stand out like the Northern Lights.

Father,
May we reflect Your light and beauty – like the Northern Lights. Amen.

March 10

Loving Warning

*Dear children, keep away from anything
that might take God's place in your hearts.*
1 John 5:21

Have you ever asked your child not to touch something? When children are toddlers, we train them not to touch electrical outlets. As they grow older and attend summer camp, we urge them to stay away from poison ivy. In their teen years, we warn them to abstain from drugs. Why do we caution them? Because we love them and want the best for them! We want them to keep away from things that could harm them.

It's good to remember that God deals with us that way too. Because He loves us and desires to have a relationship with us, He wants us to keep away from anything that might threaten that relationship or bring harm to us. His warnings flow out of His loving heart.

Father,
Thank You for Your protective love and consistent care. May we be careful not to jeopardize our loving relationship with You. Amen.

March 11

Spring Rains

Rejoice in the LORD your God! For the rain He sends demonstrates His faithfulness. Once more the autumn rains will come, as well as the rains of spring.

Joel 2:23

It is almost springtime in Chicago! Yesterday was an amazing day, reaching 75° F (24° C) with abundant sunshine. Today, it's supposed to rain, probably a long, gentle spring rain. The rain will wash away the remaining dirt and debris left from winter, leaving things fresh and clean. Winter is long in this part of the world, so when milder days arrive, they come filled with hope and a promise of better days to come.

I remind myself that the cold winters, filled with rain and snow, make it possible for abundant trees and foliage to burst forth in coming weeks. God has given us seasons to remind us of His eternal faithfulness. Spring rains are refreshing!

Lord,
The changing seasons remind me of Your great faithfulness. How glad I am that You never change – You are the Lord our God! Amen.

March 12

The Humble Donkey

Rejoice, O people of Zion! Shout in triumph, O people
of Jerusalem! Look, your King is coming to you.
He is righteous and victorious, yet He is humble,
riding on a donkey – riding on a donkey's colt.
Zechariah 9:9

Regardless of what we might think of the donkey, the animal enjoyed a rich history in the Bible. The poorest of families usually owned a donkey, but kings also rode them in royal ceremony. While horses were associated with armies and conquests, donkeys were associated with peace.

Zechariah looked into the future and predicted the coming Messiah's donkey. Jesus fulfilled that prophecy, when he rode into Jerusalem on a donkey – the apex of that animal's appearance in the Bible. The donkey signified the humility of Jesus as He bent to the will of His Father. Here was not the conquering king the Jews were seeking, but Jesus, the humble and obedient servant King.

Lord,
Help me, like Jesus, to be quick to serve rather than ready to rule. Amen.

March 13

Palm Branches

*The next day, the news that Jesus was on the way to
Jerusalem swept through the city. A large crowd of
Passover visitors took palm branches and went down the
road to meet Him. They shouted ,"Praise God! Blessings
on the one who comes in the name of the Lord!"*

John 12:12-13

Palm trees appeared early in the Bible, carved on
various walls of the Temple. They were also found
on pottery, coins, and sculptures from early periods
of Middle Eastern history.

The palm branch symbolized rejoicing, triumph,
and victory. It is no surprise, then, that the people
of Israel selected palm branches to strew across the
road ahead of Jesus' triumphal entry into Jerusalem.
Jesus' ultimate triumph, though, is best seen in the
book of Revelation where a vast crowd, too great to
count, stands before His throne with palm branches
in their hands, worshiping the King of kings.

Lord,
I look forward to the day when I, too, will hold a palm branch,
shouting, "Salvation comes from our God who sits on the
throne and from the Lamb." Amen.

March 14

Betrayal

*Jesus answered, "Die for Me? I tell you the truth,
Peter – before the rooster crows tomorrow morning,
you will deny three times that you even know Me."*
John 13:38

How boldly Peter pronounced his intentions to follow Jesus! "I'm ready to die for you!" Imagine how
stunned Peter must have been when Jesus told him
the truth. Peter probably believed he would stand
with Jesus till the end.

His denial is a warning to all of us who believe
our commitment to Christ is strong and impenet-
rable. When our attitude reflects such arrogance, we
become vulnerable to our weaknesses in the midst
of our reckless bravado.

Like the disciples, we sometimes fall away from
Christ when things become difficult. But there is
hope. Jesus' death and resurrection was the remedy
for Peter's weakness and denials, and it's the remedy for ours too.

Lord,
Thank You that You know all things. You know our weaknesses and failures. Thank You that You do not abandon us, but
remain with us forever. Amen.

March 15

God's Plan

Then Simon Peter drew a sword and slashed off the right ear of Malchus, the high priest's slave. But Jesus said to Peter, "Put your sword back into its sheath. Shall I not drink from the cup of suffering the Father has given Me?"
John 18:10-11

Immediately after Jesus was betrayed and arrested, one of Jesus' disciples attempted to defend Him. Peter reached for his sword and took off the right ear of the high priest's slave. In response to Peter's impulsive action, Jesus told him to put away his sword, and proceeded to heal Malchus's ear (Luke 22:51).

Jesus knew that in order for God's plan of salvation to be accomplished, He needed to submit to death on a cross. He chose the cup of suffering instead of the sword, submitting to God's will instead of resisting.

At times in our lives when we face the possibility of suffering as a result of following Christ, we should trust God the way Jesus did. Are we willing to submit to God's plan?

March 16

Father,
Like Jesus, may we have hearts that trust Your plan. Amen.

Loving Authority

*Jesus came and told His disciples, "I have been given
all authority in heaven and on earth. Therefore,
go and make disciples of all the nations ... Teach these
new disciples to obey all the commands I have given you.
And be sure of this: I am with you always."*
Matthew 28:18-20

"This is Jesus, King of the Jews." The sign above
Jesus' cross was not a declaration. It was a mockery.
The jeering men around Jesus had stripped Him,
dressed Him in a scarlet robe, woven a crown of
thorns for His head, taunted Him, spat on Him, and
crucified Him.

If I had been mocked the way Jesus was mocked,
I would have wanted to take revenge on the jeering
crowd after I had come back to life. But after Jesus'
resurrection, when all authority was given to
Him, what did He want His disciples to do? Not
take revenge, but go and share the Good News of
forgiveness with the whole world. What a loving
Savior!

Gracious Savior,
We are awed by Your loving and unselfish ways. Please help
us to follow Your example. Amen.

March 17

Service of Darkness

At noon, darkness fell across the whole land until three o'clock. At about three o'clock, Jesus called out with a loud voice, "Eli, Eli, lema sabachthani?" which means "My God, My God, why have You abandoned Me?"

Matthew 27:45-46

My church holds a solemn and moving service on the evening of Good Friday known as a Service of Darkness. It helps the congregation enter into the betrayal, suffering, and abandonment of Christ's crucifixion. During the course of the service, lights and candles that have been burning are gradually extinguished. Finally, there is complete darkness, save perhaps one small candle. The growing darkness helps us experience the sense of gloom as evil appears to triumph over good.

The service ends, and we leave in complete silence as we experience grief over the death of Jesus. It is an unfinished service. No benediction, no music, no light. Only silence.

March 18

Dear Jesus,
It was our sin that put You on that cross — our self-centeredness and our rebellion. We have no greater friend than You. Amen.

Already Solved

*Very early on Sunday morning ... they went to the tomb. On
the way they were asking each other, "Who will roll away
the stone for us from the entrance to the tomb?"
But as they arrived, they looked up and saw that the stone,
which was very large, had already been rolled aside.*
Mark 16:2-4

Before Mary Magdalene, Salome, and Mary even
knew there was such a thing as Resurrection morning, the women thought their immediate problem
was how to roll away the stone in front of Jesus'
tomb. What they discovered, though, was that the
problem Jesus had just solved was much bigger
than the problem they thought they had. Jesus had
just dealt with the problem of sin and death.

By taking our sins upon Himself and conquering death, Jesus made it possible for us to receive
forgiveness. Like the women at the tomb, we see
our problems differently when we realize what
Jesus has already accomplished on our behalf.

Father,
Because You have dealt with our biggest problems – sin and
death – we can trust You for the smaller problems we face
today. Amen.

March 19

The Day of Resurrection

"Why are you looking among the dead for someone who is alive? He isn't here! He is risen from the dead!"
Luke 24:5-6

The glow of the rising sun on the horizon ... the chill of the morning air ... such was the backdrop for the women who went to Jesus' tomb a few days after His crucifixion. It was in this setting that the women discovered that things had been forever changed.

Darkness had changed to light. Death had changed to life. The women were stunned and terrified by the angel's appearance and good news! "He is risen from the dead!" He is risen indeed!

None of us has ever faced a crisis deeper than death. The reality of Christ's resurrection brings new hope for us all. In His life we live, and are raised from our deadness.

Hallelujah! Praise God!
You have reached out to us and conquered our ultimate fear and enemy. Death and defeat have been swallowed up in Your greatest victory! Because You live, so will we! Hallelujah! Amen.

I Told You So

Then the angel spoke to the women. "Don't be afraid!" he said. "I know you are looking for Jesus, who was crucified. He isn't here! He is risen from the dead, just as He said would happen. Come, see where His body was lying."

Matthew 28:5-6

It was a sad day when my neighbor called to say that my family's pet had been struck and killed by a car. "Remember how I told you," my neighbor said to her children, "that if you don't look both ways before you cross the street you might get hit by a car?" She had warned her children before, but now they *believed* her!

After Jesus' death, when Mary and Mary Magdalene went to visit Jesus' tomb and found it empty, the angel said, "He isn't here – He's risen, just as He said." Jesus had said it – many times – but now they believed Him! Since Jesus rose from the dead just as He said He would, we too can believe that He will accomplish everything else He has promised.

Father,
Thank You that we can be confident in the belief that You mean what You say. Amen.

March 21

Walking with Jesus

*That same day two of Jesus' followers were walking
to the village of Emmaus. As they walked along they
were talking about everything that had happened ... Jesus
Himself suddenly came and began walking with them.
But God kept them from recognizing Him ... They stopped
short, sadness written across their faces.*

Luke 24:13-17

Jesus cared deeply about the two disciples who were traveling to Emmaus. In the midst of their discouragement and confusion, Jesus came to them, even though they didn't recognize Him.

He wanted to encourage them, and He did it with the Word of God. As He spoke about God's faithfulness to people scattered throughout the Old Testament, the disciples' hearts were warmed, and their eyes were opened. They were walking with Jesus!

No matter where we are in our journey, Jesus is ready to nourish us with His Word and His presence. He wants to walk with us, too!

March 22

Lord,
Thank You that my journey through life is not hidden to You.
Give me faith to see the reality of Your presence. Amen.

Come for Breakfast!

"Now come and have some breakfast!" Jesus said.
None of the disciples dared to ask Him, "Who are You?"
They knew it was the Lord.
John 21:12

The sun crept over the horizon, smoke drifted up from the fire, and the aroma of freshly cooked fish hung in the air. In the midst of the disciples' disappointment and loss, some of them had decided to go back to fishing.

That's where the risen Lord came to meet them – right where they were. He did not shame them for their sadness or wear-iness or ignorance. Instead He approached them, provided for them, and nourished them.

Whatever our experience, whatever our need, Jesus comes to meet us. Maybe we're not even looking for Him, but He longs to be a part of our lives. Jesus offers Himself to us in all His fullness. We need but eyes of faith and hearts of belief.

Lord,
Sometimes I live my life as though You are still in the tomb. Help me to see that You long to be with me and nourish me at the deepest level of my need. Amen.

March 23

Refreshingly Honest

*Save me, O God, for the floodwaters are up
to my neck. Deeper and deeper I sink into the mire;
I can't find a foothold. I am in deep water,
and the floods overwhelm me.*

Psalm 69:1-2

If you feel like you're drowning emotionally and you're looking for some perspective, consider reading through the Psalms. Refreshingly honest, the Psalms assure us that we're not alone in our situations or our emotions. They offer us hope. If you're confused or struggling with complicated feelings, you might be encouraged at how much you can identify with the psalmists. You might also be surprised by how 'understood' you feel as you read them.

There's something in the Psalms for just about any kind of circumstance or emotion. It's no wonder that John Calvin called the Psalms "an anatomy of all the parts of the soul."

Understanding Father,
It feels so good to know that others before me have confidently poured out their souls to You. Please help me in my time of need. Amen.

March 24

God Is in Control

"I am the Alpha and the Omega – the beginning and the end," says the Lord God. "I am the one who is, who always was, and who is still to come – the Almighty One."
Revelation 1:8

Who is the most powerful and influential person you know? The South African Ambassador to the US? The President of Fellowes, Inc.? The Administrator of the US Environmental Protection Agency? As much power as these people presently hold, each of them was helpless on the day he was born and each will be helpless on the day he dies – just like the rest of us.

God is very different, though. Almighty God – who we can have a relationship with through faith in Christ – has complete power and control over everything, including time. He always was, He presently is, and He always will be. Whatever limitations you may be facing today, be encouraged that God Almighty has no limitations. He is in complete control, and He cares about you.

Lord God,
Thank You that You are in control. Please help us to trust our time constraints to Your limitless power. Amen.

March 25

A Way for Justice

O LORD, hear my plea for justice.
Listen to my cry for help.
Pay attention to my prayer, for it comes from honest lips.
Psalm 17:1

Where do pleas for justice come from? Usually, from the mouths of people who have been treated unjustly. Whether it was being bullied as a child, cheated in a business transaction, or betrayed in a relationship, injustices have probably caused most of us pain at one point or another.

Since Jesus knows all things, He understands the injustices of life perfectly. When He hung on the cross for our sins, He did not cry out for justice. Instead, He took the burden of all the world's injustices on Himself. It's comforting to remember that God – the only One in the universe who completely understands justice and injustice – is also the One who listens to our prayers, and who, ultimately, has made things right.

Lord,
Thank You that You have overcome all that is wrong and un-fair in the world. Help us turn to You in faith for strength and courage today. Amen.

March 26

A Great Party

"But his father said to the servants, 'Quick!
Bring the finest robe ... Get a ring ... and sandals ...
We must celebrate with a feast, for this son of mine ...
was lost, but now he is found.' So the party began."
Luke 15:22-24

The story of the Prodigal Son is one of the best known parables in the Bible. In the culture of that day, the son's demand for his share of the inheritance was a great insult to the father. Requesting his father's money and announcing that he was leaving, the son was in essence wishing that his father was dead. The son returns home however. In his joy, the father lavishes affection on the lost son who had been found by giving him a robe, sandals, and a ring – all symbols of sonship.

The return of the son is important, but the focus of the story is the father's joy. Our heavenly Father, whose love for us is deep and unending, shows His joy over our repentance too. Let the party begin!

Father,
Help us to remember that Your love for us is deep and never ending. Thank You for Your joy over our repentance. Amen.

March 27

No Other God

So remember this and keep it firmly in mind: The LORD is God both in heaven and on earth, and there is no other.

Deuteronomy 4:39

Before Moses led the children of Israel out of Egypt, God used dreadful plagues to demonstrate the impotence of Egypt's gods. Later, He took the Israelites to Mt. Sinai where He gave Moses the Ten Commandments.

The first commandment states, "You must not have any other god but Me." To us in modern times, worship of the ancient gods may seem puzzling or absurd, but today's culture has its own idols of money, sex, and power. We, too, are tempted to bow to these gods. What God wants, though, is for us to pursue Him more than anything else. God knows that we will be most content when we are totally devoted to Him.

Lord,
Give me the passion to turn away from all that would dilute my love for You. Help me to follow Jesus' command to love You with all my heart, my soul, and my mind. Amen.

March 28

Winter Is Past

The winter is past, and the rains are over and gone.
The flowers are springing up, the season of singing birds
has come, and the cooing of turtledoves fills the air.
Song of Songs 2:11-12

Some of my family's fondest memories were made
on our annual spring treks to Florida. Our family of
five usually loaded up the car, anchored lawn chairs
to the roof rack, and headed south. The snow of
Chicago eventually disappeared, yielding buds on
the trees and finally giving way to palm trees and
lush growth. As we drove further south, our spirits were refreshed by the scent of orange blossoms.
Not only were the sights and smells different –
the sounds were different, too. Birds were singing!
It was as if the earth had been refreshed and a sense
of renewal was in the air.

The coming of spring reminds me that God is
always ready to refresh my spirit by the presence
of His Spirit.

Lord,
Thank You for lessons I see in Your world around me. Nothing
escapes Your care, and all things sing Your praises if I have eyes
to see it! Amen.

The Tent of Meeting

*It was Moses' practice to take the Tent of Meeting
and set it up some distance from the camp.
Inside the Tent of Meeting, the L*ORD *would speak
to Moses face to face, as one speaks to a friend.*

Exodus 33:7, 11

The thirty-third chapter of Exodus describes a special tent that Moses set up to meet with God. When they met together inside the tent, God spoke to Moses face to face. "Wouldn't it be wonderful to have a place like that?" we might say.

Jesus made it possible for us to have such an experience when He came to earth. No longer do we have to go to a tent, or to the Temple in Jerusalem. Rather, He came to reside within us. Paul the apostle wrote that *we* are now the temple – the residence of the Holy Spirit. Our sighs and our prayers are always heard because God is with us, and Jesus promised that He would never leave us.

Lord,
Thank You that You are not limited to a special location like a tent. Best of all, Your Spirit wants to take up residence within us. Amen.

March 30

Dead Bones Live

"Dry bones, listen to the word of the Lord! This is what the Sovereign Lord says: Look! I am going to put breath into you and make you live again! I will put breath into you, and you will come to life. Then you will know that I am the Lord."

Ezekiel 37:4-6

In this strange prophecy, Ezekiel the prophet was carried away to a valley of dry bones. There, God gave him an illustration of what He was going to do for the people of Israel. He would resurrect their dead, sinful lives, and energize them again by the power of His life-giving Spirit. The good news is that God continues to do this today.

I have a friend who professed faith in Christ but inwardly had a spirit as dead as the dry bones Ezekiel saw. One day, the sin that had filled her life was exposed. Her confession was like the "rattling" that Ezekiel heard when the bones in the valley began to come alive. By the resurrection power of God, my friend experienced a spiritual transformation, and those who know her see that it is the work of God.

Lord,
We're grateful that Your resurrection power brings life. Amen.

March 31

April

Training for Life

No discipline is enjoyable while it is happening – it's
painful! But afterward there will be a peaceful harvest
of right living for those who are trained in this way.
Hebrews 12:11

One of my friends likes to run marathons; grueling races of more than twenty-six miles. She competed in the Nashville Marathon a while ago, a run that included extra challenges of hills and valleys. My friend spent months training for the marathon, and her preparation included running in unpleasant conditions – the Chicago winter being one of them. Training can be painful, but my friend's preparation paid off. When she ran the Nashville Marathon, she achieved her best time ever!

God's discipline in our lives is sometimes painful too. But we have the assurance that when we have completed our training, we will see evidence of His work in our lives and we can anticipate our reward.

Lord,
Help me to keep my eyes on the finish line, and remember that Your training is for Your honor and my good. Amen.

April 1

New Purpose

"Look! I stand at the door and knock. If you hear
My voice and open the door, I will come in,
and we will share a meal together as friends."
Revelation 3:20

The president of a prosperous investment firm was
concerned about a young man in his church who
was struggling with depression, and invited him
out for lunch. Over the meal, he suggested that the
young man come to work with him, assuring him
that he would look out for him. Being invited into
that relationship brought a new sense of purpose
and hope to the young man.

God has invited each of us to embark on a life-
changing relationship that is as close as the door of
our hearts. If we leave Christ standing on the outside of our hearts, we will be hungry and poor. But
if we invite Him in, we will find ourselves living
with new purpose and hope. Have you opened the
door?

Father,
We're grateful that a relationship with You gives us purpose.
Amen.

April 2

Deeply Discouraged

*Why am I discouraged? Why is my heart so sad? I will
put my hope in God! I will praise Him again – my
Savior and my God! Now I am deeply discouraged, but I will
remember You – even from distant Mount Hermon,
the source of the Jordan, from the land of Mount Mizar.*

Psalm 42:5

Sometimes we feel like we are the only ones who
struggle with heaviness of heart. How gracious,
then, that the writer who penned Psalm 42 informs
us that we are not the only ones who get depressed.
He did, too. I appreciate the straight-forward way
that he expressed his feelings: "Now I am deeply
discouraged." He didn't stop there, though. Using
the little word *but*, he switched gears to something
that had probably helped him on similar occasions.
"But I will remember You."

It's good for us to remember how God was helpful to people in the Bible, and how He has been
helpful to us. Memories of God's faithfulness in the
past can bring us encouragement in the present.

Father,
In our discouragement, may we remember You and put our
hope in You. Amen.

April 3

Blessed Neediness

Then Jesus turned to His disciples and said, "God blesses
you who are poor, for the Kingdom of God is yours. God
blesses you who are hungry now, for you will be satisfied. God
blesses you who weep now, for in due time you will laugh."
Luke 6:20-21

Are you struggling with a lack of resources finan-
cially, physically, or emotionally? Are you feeling
dissatisfied with your life the way it is? According
to Jesus' Sermon on the Mount, that's not a bad
place to be. It actually fits the description of what
Jesus labels a life of blessing.

   Jesus was not saying to His disciples that pov-er-
ty, hunger, or tears were good things on their own.
After all, He performed many miracles to attend to
such woes. Jesus was addressing our inner attitudes
of spiritual neediness, saying that those needs push
us towards a personal relationship with God – our
biggest need. We are blessed the most not when we
"get" or "do", but when we need God.

Father,
We are a needy bunch. May our needs push us towards You.
Amen.

April 4

Star Gazing

[God] spreads out the heavens like a curtain and makes His tent from them. Look up into the heavens. Who created all the stars? He brings them out like an army, one after another, calling each by its name. Because of His great power and incomparable strength, not a single one is missing.

Isaiah 40:22, 26

Recently, my husband's business took him to New Zealand. While traveling south toward Wellington, he stayed at a hotel near the foot of several volcanoes in the Tongariro National Park. After dinner, Jim decided to wander out under the stars since the area was far from city lights. When he looked up into the sky, he literally gasped at what he saw. The Milky Way washed through the center of the sky, and the unfamiliar constellations of the southern hemisphere prompted his worship. Never in all his life had he seen stars so bright and distinct.

Experiences like that remind us of God's power, strength, and care – and there's no charge for admission!

Lord,
It is a wonder that while You created all the stars and constellations, You also made us. Thank You! Amen.

April 5

Take Courage

Jesus came toward them, walking on the water ...
They were all terrified ... But Jesus spoke to them at once.
"Don't be afraid," He said. "Take courage! I am here!"
Then He climbed into the boat, and the wind stopped.
They were totally amazed ...
Their hearts were too hard to take it in.
Mark 6:48-52

After Jesus fed over 5,000 people with five loaves of bread and two fish, His disciples encountered a storm on the Sea of Galilee. We might surmise that anyone who had just seen Jesus perform one miracle would think, *A terrible storm? No problem!* That's not how the disciples responded, though. They were terrified.

We sometimes respond similarly to storms in our lives. We panic. We try to take charge of the situation. When we face our own storms, will we believe that Jesus, the Son of God, really can come to our aid and help us? Nothing in the whole world is outside of Jesus' authority.

Powerful God,
We panic so easily, even though we know You have helped us before. Please give us courage to trust You. Amen.

April 6

He Is Coming

Even the wilderness and desert will be glad in those days.
The wasteland will rejoice and blossom with spring crocuses.
With this news, strengthen those who have tired hands,
and encourage those who have weak knees. Say to those
with fearful hearts, "Be strong, and do not fear,
for your God ... is coming to save you."
Isaiah 35:1, 3-4

The crab apple tree must be starting to bloom, I thought. *I'm sneezing a lot!* I walked to the front window and looked out at the tree. Sure enough, buds were beginning to blossom. That's a hopeful sign in Chicago, where the winters are long. Seasons of our lives are sometimes like those long, dark winters. Thankfully, God has promised that there are better things ahead.

Someday, He will return for His children that He has redeemed. Then, blind eyes will be opened, deaf ears will be unplugged and lame legs will leap like a deer. Buds on trees are some of God's reminders that never-ending joy awaits those who trust Him.

Father,
Thank You that there is joy ahead. Please strengthen us while we wait. Amen.

April 7

Catch the Foxes

"Catch all the foxes, those little foxes, before they ruin the vineyard of love, for the grapevines are blossoming!"
Song of Songs 2:15

If a vineyard isn't protected, foxes can quickly and easily destroy valuable produce, feeding on the vegetation and fruits available to them. Once foxes are discovered, though, fences and gates can be installed to protect the vineyard. Like vineyards, marriages need protection too. When things like laziness, immodesty, debt, or pornography threaten our marriages, they need to be exposed and chased away, before they spoil and ruin the vineyard of love.

Unfortunately, foxes surface from time to time in most marriages. Wise husbands and wives move quickly to deal with the problems, protecting their relationship with appropriate boundaries, fences, and gates. If you are married, what steps will you take to protect your marriage from foxes that threaten to ruin your vineyard?

April 8

Father,
Please help us to identify and take action against problems in our marriages. Thank You that You help us to do this. Amen.

Power and Love

He brought Israel out of Egypt ... He acted with
a strong hand and powerful arm ... Give thanks
to Him who parted the Red Sea ... He led Israel
safely through, His faithful love endures forever.
Psalm 136:11-14

At times in our lives when things feel out of control, it's good to be reminded that God is not passive. God has always been active, He is active now, and He always will be active.

In order for us to trust Him in the present, it's helpful for us to remember what He's done in the past. "He brought Israel out of Egypt. He acted with a strong and powerful arm. He parted the Red Sea. He led Israel safely through." God was both their Shepherd and their powerful Savior. He is no less powerful or active today than He was in Moses' day. Just as God led His people with power then, He still leads us with power today.

Father,
Thank You that You are a powerful and loving Shepherd.
Amen.

April 9

Radiant Light

"If you are filled with light, with no dark corners,
then your whole life will be radiant,
as though a floodlight were filling you with light."
Luke 11:36

Some of you probably have floodlights on the sides or backs of your houses or apartments. Floodlights give off steady and intense beams of light that spread over a wide area. Installed on corners and walls of buildings, they offer a measure of safety and security. Floodlights are also useful to photographers, who don't want shadows in their pictures.

Throughout the Bible, light represents God, because God is light. When we live in relationship with God, He shines the light of His truth into our hearts like a floodlight. His light offers us safety and security, eliminating dark corners and lurking shadows. Christ's presence in our lives brings safety and sparkle.

Father,
We're thankful for Your light that chases darkness out of our hearts. We want to walk in Your light. Amen.

April 10

A Dangerous Trap

Fearing people is a dangerous trap,
but trusting the LORD means safety.
Proverbs 29:25

One morning I rounded the corner of my laundry room and caught a glimpse of a mouse. First, I screamed. Then, I decided to set a trap. When enticed by peanut butter, oats, or chocolate (mice aren't really that fond of cheese), they go for the bait, not realizing the danger ahead.

Some of us do the same when we charge right into the trap of fearing people. Constant fear of people is a quagmire, and getting out requires help. Looking to God for security is the place to begin. The more we look up and find security in our relationship with God, the less power fear will have over us. Trusting God helps us avoid the dangerous trap of fear.

Father,
Sometimes we act more fearful of people than we do of mice. We're grateful that You help us overcome our fears. Amen.

April 11

Good Regret

*For the kind of sorrow God wants us to experience
leads us away from sin and results in salvation.
There's no regret for that kind of sorrow. But worldly
sorrow, which lacks repentance, results in spiritual death.*

2 Corinthians 7:10

Most of us have regrets – things we feel uneasy about, things we feel sorrow for, or things we look back on and wish we had handled differently. When it comes to regrets, the difference between immaturity and maturity is in the way we process them. People who are angry, defensive, and sorry only for getting caught lack true repentance and often repeat whatever it is they are 'sorry' about.

Those who feel genuine remorse, though – who repent of their sin and humbly depend on God's help to turn away from that sin, will grow and thrive. There's no regret for that kind of regret!

Father,
Sorrow that leads us away from sin is one of Your gracious gifts. Please help us to see it from Your perspective. Amen.

April 12

Advertise God's Power

Now that I am old and gray, do not abandon me, O God.
Let me proclaim Your power to this new generation.
Psalm 71:18

Some things about growing older aren't appealing;
wrinkling skin, graying hair, and deteriorating eye-
sight. However, other aspects of growing older are
attractive; wisdom acquired through the ups and
downs of life, evidences of God's faithfulness, and
opportunities to share those things with others.

Even though there's a tremendous emphasis in
our culture on looking young, God assures us that
He doesn't abandon us as we grow older. In reality,
we have special opportunities for serving Him as
we mature. We have unique occasions to tell those
around us how God's power has been evident to us –
meeting our physical needs, freeing us from bon-
dage to sin, and helping us in our relationships.
How might we share those thoughts with others
today?

Father,
Thank You for not abandoning us as we grow older. May we
snatch opportunities to tell younger generations about Your
power. Amen.

April 13

Tulips for a Time

All men are like grass, and all their glory is like the
flowers of the field. The grass withers and the
flowers fall ... but the word of our God stands forever.
Isaiah 40:6, 8 (NIV)

My husband and I recently traveled to Holland at the height of tulip season. We visited Keukenhof, a magnificent park full of flower gardens and have never seen a more stunning presentation of tulips. Keukenhof is open only during the months of April and May – the park is closed from June to March. After the flowers have withered and fallen, only the memory of their brief glory is left behind.

Isaiah shouted that although flowers fade, and people fade just like flowers, God's Word does not. It stands forever, with a stunning beauty and strength that enriches us as we read it.

Lord,
In all their glory, flowers cannot compare to the magnificence and endurance of Your Word! Give us the wisdom and discipline to explore and enjoy it as we would the most beautiful of earthly parks. Amen.

April 14

Faithful Legacy

*Naomi took the baby and cuddled him to her breast.
And she cared for him as if he were her own.
The neighbor women said, "Now at last Naomi has a
son again!" And they named him Obed. He became
the father of Jesse and the grandfather of David.*
Ruth 4:16-17

Ruth, a young Moabite widow, chose to follow her widowed mother-in-law, Naomi back to Bethlehem. She also made a choice to follow God. After Naomi and Ruth arrived in Bethlehem, God graciously provided food and shelter for them. He also provided a new husband for Ruth. Ruth ended up marrying kind Boaz and having a son, Obed, who brought great joy to his parents and to Naomi.

Although Ruth didn't know it at the time, her son Obed would eventually become the grandfather of King David. That meant that Jesus was born into Ruth's family line! Choices we make to obey God now extend far beyond anything we could ever imagine. Faithfulness now leaves a rich legacy later.

Father,
May we be faithful to You today. We want to leave a good legacy for those who follow us. Amen.

April 15

Growing and Thriving

All the believers devoted themselves to the apostles'
teaching, and to fellowship, and to sharing in meals
(including the Lord's Supper), and to prayer.

Acts 2:42

I wasn't pleased with the mediocre growth of the flowers around my house. In comparison to the flowers my mother planted around her house, mine looked anemic. "I have a formula," said my mom, "that has produced thriving flowers for years. Mix 2 cups bone meal, 1 cup Epson salts, and 1 cup sugar into a tin can. Then, place one tablespoon of the mixture into each hole in the soil where a plant will grow. Use these ingredients, and your plants and flowers will flourish!"

Acts 2:42 gives us a formula of sorts – a formula that shows us how we can grow as Christian believers. Combine God's truth, fellowship, shared meals – including the Lord's Supper and prayer – and we will see growth. It's been a proven formula for centuries.

Father,
We're grateful that You left us specific guidelines on how to grow strong. Amen.

April 16

Focus on the Heart

Since everything around us is going to be destroyed like this,
what holy and godly lives you should live,
looking forward to the day of God and hurrying it along.
2 Peter 3:11-12

The old medical building that I've gone to for almost thirty years will soon be torn down. It's about to be replaced with a state-of-the-art building right next door to it, and the employees of the clinic can't wait to move in. The last time I was in the old building I noticed that the carpet was fraying, and I reasoned that the owners must not want to spend much money on upkeep right now. At this point, their money is better spent on the patients and technology inside the building.

It's important for us to make similar evaluations for our lives. We're wise to invest our time and efforts on matters of the heart, as opposed to temporary, outward things that don't last. What will we focus on today?

Father,
In spite of all the things that clamor for our time and energy, we want to focus on matters of the heart. We need Your wisdom to help us. Amen.

April 17

Speak God's Word

"Stand up, son of man," said the voice. "I want to speak with you." The Spirit came into me as He spoke, and He set me on my feet. I listened carefully to His words. "Son of man," He said, "I am sending you to the nation of Israel, a rebellious nation that has rebelled against Me."

Ezekiel 2:1-3

William Tyndale, an English reformer from the 1500s, felt called to translate the Bible into English so that common people could understand what God was saying to them. During the perilous days of the 16th century, Tyndale faced great opposition from the official church of the day and was eventually burned at the stake for translating God's Word into the common language.

Thousands of years earlier, Ezekiel was called by God. God told him that the nation he prophesied to would rebel at his words, yet God would turn the hearts of those He called through the hearing of His Word. We can understand God's Word today because of faithful men like Ezekiel and Tyndale.

Lord,
Give me the courage to speak Your Word whenever You give me the opportunity. Amen.

April 18

The Only Way

Jesus told him, "I am the way, the truth, and the life.
No one can come to the Father except through Me."
John 14:6-7

My sister-in-law, Joanie, recently taught her computer class how to download photos from a digital camera. Her students commented that the "USB" plug fits into the camera only one way – the way the designer made it to work.

Joanie was reminded that despite the cultural trend to embrace the notion that there are many ways to God, Jesus made an exclusive claim. Truth by nature is exclusive. We cannot invent truth; we discover truth and live by it.

Jesus offers everyone the opportunity to find life in Him and live by His ways. His truth is free to all. But He is the only one who can make the exclusive claim of being Truth Himself.

Lord Jesus,
Keep me from rebelling against Your exclusive claims. Help me to embrace You and live by Your truth in all that I do. Amen.

April 19

Repentance Is a Gift

*Plant the good seeds of righteousness, and you
will harvest a crop of love. Plow up the hard ground
of your hearts, for now is the time to seek the LORD, that
He may come and shower righteousness upon you.*

Hosea 10:12

Before we plant beans or tomatoes in the spring,
the soil in our garden needs some attention. Using
a spade or a roto-tiller, we rid the dirt of weeds and
prepare the soil for the seeds we're about to plant.

Just as hard soil on the ground needs to be
cultivated, hearts of sin and rebellion need to be
cultivated, too.

As the plow is to soil on the ground, so repentance
is to the soil of our hearts. When we admit our sins
and ask God's forgiveness, His righteousness can
grow in our hearts.

Allowing the plow of repentance to do its good
work brings a promised harvest – love. Repentance
isn't something to avoid – it's something to embrace.

Father,
Thank You that repentance makes it possible for good things
to grow in our hearts. Amen.

April 20

Awakening Love

Promise me, O women of Jerusalem, by the gazelles and wild deer, not to awaken love until the time is right.
Song of Songs 2:7

Physical intimacy is to be awakened only at the right time – when a man and woman are husband and wife. It is not to be awakened at the wrong time – when a man and woman are not yet married or when they are married to someone else.

In the context of marriage, love that is awakened or aroused is a gift from God. Outside of that context, it produces all kinds of pain and problems for the man, the woman, their families, and generations yet to come.

Each of us is wise to think of ways we can avoid arousing physical intimacy in inappropriate relationships, and how we will work toward arousing love in our marriage.

Father,
We are grateful that You set up boundaries to protect us. Help us to honor You by honoring and protecting those boundaries. Amen.

Power Is Available

*Pray that you will understand the incredible
greatness of God's power for us who believe Him.
This is the same mighty power that raised Christ
from the dead and seated Him at God's right hand.*

Ephesians 1:19-20

Imagine that you relocate a woman from the jungles
of Papau New Guinea to Chicago, and out-fitted her
new home with all sorts of appliances. What if you
visited her several days later and found her in the
backyard, cooking dinner over a fire? You'd think,
'I need to tell her there's a coffee pot, toaster, stove,
and refrigerator in the house that will help make
her life a lot easier.'

Sometimes believers in Christ need similar
reminders. Power is available to us to help with
all the challenges of life! God's mighty power that
raised Christ from the dead is the same power that
brings us God's grace, peace, understanding, and
hope. These gifts are available to us when we place
our faith in Christ.

God,
We praise You for Your power that raised Jesus from the dead.
Thank You that You share that power with us. Amen.

April 22

Sustaining Care

For the angel of the LORD is a guard;
he surrounds and defends all who fear Him.
Psalm 34:7
"My God sent His angel to shut the lions' mouths,
so that they would not hurt me."
Daniel 6:22

Many of us have mourned the loss of family mem-bers or friends, some of whom seem to have been taken much too early. These situations are impossible to make sense of and are difficult to accept.

Both Daniel and the psalmist knew that they would eventually die. We all do. But they acknowledged times when they could have died and praised God for His care in keeping them alive. They must have figured that God still had purposes for them to fulfill.

Yes, each of us will die. But we can trust and thank God that He has guarded us in the past and will guard us until it is His time for us to go. No one ever dies a day too soon.

Father,
Thank You for times when You have protected and sustained us – especially those times that we don't know about. Amen.

April 23

Live in Harmony

May God, who gives this patience and encouragement,
help you live in complete harmony with each other,
as is fitting for followers of Christ Jesus.
Romans 15:5

At the age of eight or nine, I discovered how much fun it was to sing in harmony. Up until that point, whether humming along with the radio or singing songs in church, I'd sung only melody. Catching on to harmony opened up a new way for me to express myself musically. It also brought me pleasure.

Just as learning to sing in harmony with others is satisfying to our ears, learning to live in harmony with others is satisfying to our hearts. Even though most relationships are challenged by discord or dissonance at times, the God who created both music and relationships will help us to live in harmony with others as we follow close to Him.

Father,
Help us to harmonize well with other Christ-followers. Amen.

April 24

Jacob's God

Joyful are those who have the God of Israel [Jacob] as their helper, whose hope is in the LORD their God.

Psalm 146:5

"I will build an altar to the God who answered my prayers when I was in distress. He has been with me wherever I have gone."

Genesis 35:3

"Just how did God help Jacob?" you might ask. During Jacob's earlier years, he didn't seem to want God's help. He grabbed for things and seemed to be good at getting what he wanted. But when Jacob's brother was planning to kill him, Jacob knew that he needed help. God granted him safety, a large family, and an abundance of flocks and herds.

Through God's protective care, Jacob learned that his father's God could be his God too. Jacob's life included blessings and hardships – just like ours. Through Jacob's experiences, we're reminded that God is with us, He helps us, and He always keeps His promises.

Father,
We need Your help, too. Amen.

April 25

Relational God

*"I will live among the people of Israel and be their God,
and they will know that I am the LORD their God.
I am the one who brought them out of the land of Egypt
so that I could live among them. I am the LORD their God."*

Exodus 29:45-46

Sometimes I scratch my head and wonder, *Why would a holy God want to have a relationship with us?* I'm not sure I'll completely understand that until I get to heaven. All through the Bible, though, it is clear that God *wants* to have a relationship with us.

In the Old Testament, the fact that God was willing to descend and live in a tent in order to be with the children of Israel, spoke volumes about His concern for them.

In the New Testament, the fact that Jesus was willing to descend, live in an earthly body and die a cruel death for our sins, demonstrated the extent of His love and concern for us. That's how much God cares about us.

Father,
We are overwhelmed by the initiative You took to pursue us.
Amen.

April 26

Creative Gifts

"You are worthy, O Lord our God, to receive glory and honor and power. For You created all things, and they exist because You created what You pleased."
Revelation 4:11

Step into the sanctuary of my church on any Sunday and you will notice festive banners. At Christmas it is especially beautiful – when red and gold banners greet all who enter. These are the creative work of Marge, a woman in my congregation, who receives compliments from people around the world.

God is the ultimate Creator, having created the world and everything in it – including you and me. We, and everything around us, exist because God imagined us, fashioned us, and brought us into being. And even better, He delights in us. More than anyone else in the universe, God is worthy – admirable, dependable and reputable – to receive more than compliments. He alone is worthy to receive glory, honor, and praise.

Lord,
You are the ultimate "creative genius"! All of our gifts come from You and flow out of Your creative source. Give us the desire to turn these gifts back to You in praise and worship. Amen.

April 27

Gentle Words

Gentle words are a tree of life;
a deceitful tongue crushes the spirit.
Proverbs 15:4

What a huge contrast between gentle words and deceitful words. Gentle words build. They are kind; "I know you're having a rough day, how can I help you?" They are peaceful; "I see that we don't agree. How can we work this out respectfully?" They are compassionate; "I'm so sorry about what happened, please let me know if there's anything I can do to help."

Deceitful words take things in the opposite direction. They crush; "I'll mislead you if I want – I like having an advantage." They demoralize; "Even if I lie to you, I expect you to tolerate it and respect me anyway." They devastate; "You're a loser – there's no hope for you!" Gentle words comfort, deceitful words crush. Gentle wins every time.

Father,
Most of us have given and received hurtful words. We want to be women of gentle words. Amen.

God's Mercy

*I knew that You are a merciful and compassionate God,
slow to get angry and filled with unfailing love.*
Jonah 4:2

When we hear the name Jonah, we usually think of the big fish that swallowed the Old Testament character who ran away from God. The story has more to it than just these two characters, though. In the book of Jonah, we see God's incredible mercy – mercy that's available to anyone who realizes her spiritual need, no matter what she's done. Jonah struggled to understand how God could extend mercy to the Ninevites, who were evil enemies of his country.

Like Jonah, we sometimes struggle to understand God's mercy to someone who is seemingly undeserving ... until we're honest enough to admit that we are undeserving too. Thankfully, God longs to forgive anyone who repents from sin and turns to Him.

Compassionate God,
Thank You for showing us mercy. Please help us to show mercy to others. Amen.

April 29

The Command of Love

Let the whole world fear the LORD, and let everyone stand in awe of Him. For when He spoke, the world began! It appeared at His command.

Psalm 33:8-9

What can you command with your voice? Dog owners can (sometimes) direct their dogs to sit. Teachers can (hopefully) call for quiet in the classroom. Coaches (often) call time-outs for their teams.

God's commands at Creation were much different. Much more than just commanding someone to do something, God actually brought the world into being. Whether we were to visit the French Alps, the Canadian Rockies, or the Maldives, God has called all of it into existence simply by the word of His command.

Despite the power of His command, though, He will not force us into loving Him. For this, He has commanded that we have a choice. Love must be free to be given, or it is not love at all.

Lord,

I stand in awe that even though You spoke the world into existence, You have given me freedom to choose my response. Help me to love You with all my heart, soul and strength. Amen.

April 30

May

Messengers

*Then I heard the Lord asking, "Whom should
I send as a messenger to this people? Who will
go for us?" I said, "Here I am. Send me."*

Isaiah 6:8

Until something goes wrong with our cell phone or
computer, we rarely think about transmitters. But
they play an important part in our communication,
sending out all kinds of information. The Old Testament prophet, Isaiah, told God that he was willing
to be one of God's transmitters – he was willing to
send out God's information.

Isaiah was a good candidate for the job, but it
wasn't because he was perfect. Since he had seen
his own sinfulness, confessed it, and received God's
forgiveness, he could be an effective transmitter
of God's truth and grace to others. When we, like
Isaiah, have seen our sin, confessed it to God, and
received His forgiveness, we can be effective transmitters too.

Father,
We're well aware of how much Your love and forgiveness have
helped us. May we share that with others. Amen.

May 1

Good News!

*Later on, after John was arrested, Jesus went into
Galilee, where He preached God's Good News.
"The time promised by God has come at last!"
He announced. "The Kingdom of God is near!
Repent of your sins and believe the Good News!"*

Mark 1:14-15

What is the best news you can imagine? That your
husband has found steady employment? That your
child's leukemia is in remission? That your parents
have been reconciled? Each of these would be considered good news and each might last for a while.

Yet the Good News that Jesus preached lasts
forever. That is what makes it Good News with
capital letters. Jesus said that those who are willing
to repent of sin (release their old way of life) and
turn to God through faith in Jesus, will realize the
best news known to mankind – forgiveness of sin,
the promise of eternal life, and the power of God's
presence. That is Good News – both now and
forever.

Father,
Thank You that Your Good News makes a difference forever.
Amen.

May 2

God Never Sleeps

He will not let you stumble; the One who
watches over you will not slumber. Indeed, He who
watches over Israel never slumbers or sleeps.

Psalm 121:3-4

When I hear the word *slumber*, I think of slumber parties I attended where little of it happened. Slumber, better known as sleep, is common to us all. It's common to animals, too. Some animals sleep differently than we do, though. Cattle, horses, and sheep can sleep while standing. Whales and dolphins – conscious breathers – sleep with only one half of their brain at a time (with one eye closed!)

God, who is totally different from us and animals, doesn't sleep at all. I can't comprehend that, since most nights I fall into bed exhausted. I'm thankful that God, who watches over me, never sleeps.

Father,
Thank You for faithfully watching over us, night and day.
Amen.

May 3

Integrity Is Delightful

The LORD detests people with crooked hearts,
but He delights in those with integrity.
Proverbs 11:20

Would you rather hear that someone delights in you ... or detests you? The writer of the Old Testament book of Proverbs set us up for that question when he compared a heart of integrity to a perverse heart. A heart of integrity is full of honesty, goodness, and purity. A perverse heart is full of corruption, evil, and deceit.

The good news is that a heart of integrity begins to grow when we accept God's forgiveness of sins through faith in Christ's death and resurrection. God is delighted when we turn away from sin and trust Christ to give us new thoughts and behaviors.

Father,
We want to please You. Give us Your strength and grace to be women of integrity. Amen.

May 4

We Are Family

Even before He made the world, God loved us
and chose us in Christ to be holy and without fault
in His eyes. God decided in advance to adopt us into
His own family by bringing us to Himself
through Jesus Christ. This is what He wanted
to do, and it gave Him great pleasure.
Ephesians 1:4-5

After the birth of our first son, my husband wrote the following entry in his journal: "When Chad was born, nothing could have prepared me for the deep love I felt for this son of mine. I knew he was mine, but I knew nothing about his personality or what his interests would be. Yet I loved him, and was prepared to die for him if need be."

My husband says that from that moment on, he understood God's love better. We are God's children by adoption, and He adopted us even though He knew our sin from the beginning of time. Knowing our sin, He still died for us. What amazing love!

Lord,
Thank You for Your incredible love for us. Amen.

May 5

Instruments of Glory

Do not let any part of your body become an
instrument of evil to serve sin. Instead, give
yourselves completely to God, for you were dead, but
now you have new life. So use your whole body
as an instrument to do what is right for the glory of God.

Romans 6:13

Shopping for a violin is a fascinating experience. As I saw and heard various instruments that had been made in places like Germany, France, and Italy, I wondered, *Who played this instrument? Where was it played? How often did it change hands?* Since violins don't make music by themselves, the sound a particular violin makes ultimately depends on the person who plays it.

People, like violins, are instruments. The quality and beauty of the music we make depends on who we give our lives to. When we present ourselves to God as His instruments to do what is right, He will accomplish good things in and through us.

God,
Thank You for the new life You have given us. We give ourselves to You, body and soul. Amen.

May 6

Night Instruction

I will bless the LORD who guides me; even at night my heart instructs me. I know the LORD is always with me. I will not be shaken, for He is right beside me.
Psalm 16:7-8

Most of us have had instructors at some point in our lives – driving instructors, swimming instructors, or piano instructors. David, the writer of Psalm 16, thought of God as his heart instructor. What a beautiful thought.

Some people pay lots of money for the services of counselors, yet there is an even better instructor – God, because He knows us better than anyone else. His truth and instruction are available at any hour of the day. In fact, when we spend time during our waking hours reading His Word and communicating with Him, He continues to instruct us even in the night hours. Imagine that. Time spent with God – our heart instructor – brings benefits to us even in our sleep!

Father,
Your Word continues to do its work in our hearts – even at night! Amen.

May 7

Accept Correction

To learn, you must love discipline;
it is stupid to hate correction.

Proverbs 12:1

"The essence of good writing," said William Zinsser, "is re-writing." Whenever I put pencil to paper, not much that I write sounds right the first time around. I rarely scribble out a sentence that doesn't need to be tinkered with. Even after I re-write, editors still make more corrections, and I welcome them.

Life is a lot like writing – full of opportunities for correction, if we're open to them. The Bible goes so far as to say that it's stupid to hate correction. So the next time someone suggests that you adjust or alter something in your life, listen carefully. The advice they're offering may be helpful for your growth and development.

Father,
Help us to accept correction with humility. Amen.

Inclusive Love

Then Peter replied, "I see very clearly that God
shows no favoritism. In every nation He accepts
those who fear Him and do what is right."
Acts 10:34-35

As children, who of us didn't hope that our teacher
might show us some partiality from time to time?
While favoritism might leave us feeling affirmed,
though, it often leaves others feeling ignored. Con-
sequently, I'm thankful that God does not show
favoritism.

In this world of approximately 200 nations, He
does not show partiality or prejudice. Rather, He
makes it clear that He is seeking the whole world –
each and every person *without exception*. In order
to experience the security and love that such im-
partiality offers, God asks that we believe in Jesus.
Anyone who does will be forgiven of their sins. It's
difficult to understand such inclusive love but God
proves it to us every day.

Father,
Thank You that Your message is for every person in every
nation. Amen.

May 9

Anger Control

Don't sin by letting anger control you.
Think about it overnight and remain silent.
Psalm 4:4

Throughout the Bible – the Psalms in particular – we observe that anger is a common emotion. Some of us express it and others repress it, but all of us feel it from time to time. The challenge is to deal with it constructively and not allow it to control or dominate us.

Remaining silent long enough to think and pray is a wise thing to do. Expressing our feelings to God is also healthy – the psalmists did that regularly. And speaking the truth in love? Though easy to neglect, it is a powerful step towards living with integrity. Thanks to the healthy principles of communication that God has given us throughout the Bible, we can avoid the destructive control of anger.

Father,
We see the destruction that anger causes both within us and around us. Please help us to deal with it properly. Amen.

May 10

Common Clay Pots

*For God, who said, "Let there be light in the darkness,"
has made this light shine in our hearts so we could
know the glory of God. We now have this light shining
in our hearts, but we ourselves are like fragile clay
jars containing this great treasure.*

2 Corinthians 4:6-7

Every year my husband and I look forward to planting our annual flowers. Chicago winters are long, so we treasure the warmth and light that comes with spring's arrival. In the first week of May, we buy a special variety of colorful Impatiens, plant them in a clay pot, and hang them on a hook near the entrance to our home.

There is nothing special about that clay pot. It is not the pot itself that is beautiful, but the splash of color planted inside it that attracts attention. The Bible says that we are like clay pots. If Christ is in us, we are containers of the grandeur of God's light and life.

Lord,
Sometimes I become self-focused, thinking it is me, "the pot" that is important. Give me the humility to display Your goodness so that others will see Your glory. Amen.

May 11

Alone with God

*After sending them home, He went up into
the hills by Himself to pray.
Night fell while He was there alone.*

Matthew 14:23

How much can you accomplish in 24 hours? In a time span of less than 24 hours, Jesus fed five thousand people (with only five loaves and two fish), walked on water, and healed everyone who touched him.

Sandwiched in between feeding the five thousand and walking on water was ... prayer. How did Jesus approach His prayer time? *Alone*, and *by Himself*. If seeking time alone to talk to God the Father was necessary for Jesus, how much more important it is for us!

Andrew Murray, a famous missionary to South Africa, wrote, "Let this be my chief object in prayer, to realize the presence of my heavenly Father. Let my goal be: 'Alone with God.'"

Father,
Jesus left us a great example. May we make time to spend alone with You, too. Amen.

May 12

Taxi Encounter

May Your ways be known throughout the earth,
Your saving power among people everywhere.
May the nations praise You, O God. Let the whole world
sing for joy, because You govern the nations with justice
and guide the people of the whole world.
Psalm 67:2-4

My husband works for an international Christian publishing company and travels all over the world. Recently, after stepping into a taxicab in Singapore, he spotted one of his company's books sitting on the car's dashboard. The driver explained that he has a ministry to the people who enter his cab. He listens to them and prays for them.

Although my husband and the cabdriver live worlds apart, the two of them connected in a meaningful way because of their mutual faith in Jesus Christ. From east to west, the gospel makes its way throughout the whole earth, turning people who were strangers into friends because they are children of the same Father God.

Lord,
Thank You that You are not limited by time and space. May we find joy in this truth today! Amen.

May 13

Firmly Rooted

I pray that from His glorious, unlimited resources
He will empower you with inner strength through
His Spirit. Then Christ will make His home
in your hearts as you trust in Him. Your roots
will grow down into God's love and keep you strong.
Ephesians 3:16-17

Do you remember studying the root systems of plants back in school? You probably learned that in order for a plant to thrive above the ground, it needs a healthy root system under the ground. If there aren't adequate amounts of oxygen, water, nutrients and warmth in the soil underneath the plant, it's impossible for stems, leaves, and flowers to sprout.

Just as roots of plants grow where the conditions are favorable, so do our hearts. When our hearts draw on God's unending love and His unlimited resources, His Spirit empowers us with stability and growth. Just as a plant's growth depends on a strong root system, so do our hearts.

May 14

Father,
We're grateful that You share Your unlimited resources with us.
Amen.

A Sure Foundation

Therefore, this is what the sovereign LORD says:
"Look! I am placing a foundation stone in Jerusalem,
a firm and tested stone. It is a precious cornerstone that is
safe to build on. Whoever believes need never be shaken."
Isaiah 28:16

My husband and I once made plans to stay at a hotel in Atlanta, GA ... until we found out that part of the hotel had collapsed. Engineers were brought in, and they discovered that the foundation of the hotel had been eroded by an underground river. By that time, Jim and I had found another hotel.

Whether we're talking buildings or lives, foundations make a difference. Establishing our lives on any basis other than Christ, whether it's money, dreams, or education, is like building on a faulty foundation. Placing our faith in Christ is a safe way to build, because Christ is the sure foundation.

God, how great You are and how glorious is Your name in all the earth. Amen.

May 15

Extreme Makeovers

*Since you have heard about Jesus and have learned
the truth that comes from Him, throw off your old
sinful nature and your former way of life. Instead, let the
Spirit renew your thoughts and attitudes. Put on your new
nature, created to be like God – truly righteous and holy.*

Ephesians 4:21-24

A silver pitcher that goes from tarnished to gleaming ... an old house transformed from shabby to chic – extreme makeovers are fun to watch. Before God's Spirit began His transforming work in us, we were in need of a makeover, too. When the Holy Spirit takes up residence in us, negative attitudes and immoral thoughts are identified and knocked down.

The demolition process doesn't happen all at once – it takes time. But as we immerse ourselves in God's Word, and allow it to sink into our hearts, His Spirit begins to renew us, giving us new thoughts and attitudes that are like God – righteous and holy. God's renovations and makeovers are a beautiful sight to behold.

Father,
The prospect of a changed life is very hopeful. We're thankful that Your Spirit can renew our thoughts and attitudes. Amen.

May 16

Honor God

Finally, dear brothers and sisters, we urge you in the name of the LORD Jesus to live in a way that pleases God, as we have taught you. You live this way already, and we encourage you to do so even more.
1 Thessalonians 4:1

During a difficult time in my life, I was struggling to make an important decision. It seemed small at the time, but small decisions tend to have big effects. While talking to a wise woman who knew the specifics of my situation, I was intrigued by the advice she offered. She didn't suggest exactly what I should or shouldn't do, but she offered me two wise words – "Honor God." That was all she said!

Those wise words helped me to put things into perspective. They are words that speak not only to actions, but to attitudes as well. When we make it our goal to please God, He will help us know how to proceed by showing us the next step.

Father,
We want to honor You in all we do. May that become the growing desire of our hearts. Amen.

May 17

Don't Lose Hope

When Jesus arrived at the official's home, He saw the noisy crowd and heard the funeral music. "Get out!" He told them. "The girl isn't dead; she's only asleep." But the crowd laughed at Him. After the crowd was put outside, however, Jesus went in and took the girl by the hand, and she stood up!

Matthew 9:23-24

When a situation around us looks dark – when a person we know seems to have ruined his or her life with things like sexual immorality, drugs, or gambling – it's very easy for us to write that person off and think, "He or she will never change. It's impossible!" It's true that some people don't change. But some do.

Just as Jesus brought a dead person back to life, He can bring new life to people in whom we have lost all hope. What seemingly impossible situations are you facing today? Be careful not to give up hope or laugh at the idea that God can do the impossible.

Father,
We're grateful that You still do impossible things. Amen.

May 18

Gossip Destroys

A gossip goes around telling secrets, but those who are trustworthy can keep a confidence.

Proverbs 11:13

It's said that back in the middle ages, a young man approached a monk, saying, "I've sinned by gossiping about someone. What should I do now?" The monk suggested that the young man put a feather on every doorstep in town, and the young man followed his directions. He came back to the monk, asking if there was anything else that he could do. "Yes, there is," said the monk. "Go back and pick up all those feathers." The young man realized that the task was impossible, because the wind would have blown the feathers all over town.

That's what gossip is like. Once it's spread, it's impossible to retrieve, and very difficult to repair. Perhaps one reason that dogs have so many friends is that they wag their tails, not their tongues!

Father,
Strengthen us to keep our tongues silent at appropriate times.
Amen.

May 19

Breaking Light

"But for you who fear My name, the Sun of Righteousness will rise with healing in His wings."
Malachi 4:2

"Because of God's tender mercy, the morning light from heaven is about to break upon us, to give light to those who sit in darkness and in the shadow of death."
Luke 1:78-79

By logging on to the Old Farmer's Almanac website, I can find out exactly what time the sun will rise in the city I live – Wheaton, Illinois. All I have to do is enter my zipcode, and *poof* – the time pops up on my computer screen.

The 'sunrise' prophesied in the Bible didn't come with exact times. Zechariah's prophetic words were spoken after four centuries of silence. Christ's cosmic appearance as the Light of the World was around the corner, and the Sun was just about to rise! With that Sunrise – the birth of Jesus – came light for our darkness and healing for our souls. And only God knew exactly when it would happen!

Father,
Seeing Your prophecies fulfilled convinces us of Your trustworthiness. Thank You for being totally dependable. Amen.

May 20

The Pivot Point

*From then on, Jesus began to preach, "Repent of your sins
and turn to God, for the Kingdom of Heaven is near."*
Matthew 4:17

From the beginning of Jesus' earthly ministry, two
words that people heard Him say again and again
were *repent* and *turn*. These same two hopeful and
straightforward words continue to speak to us today. When we repent and feel sorrow over our sin,
there is hope for us. When we turn away from sin
and selfishness – when we do an about-face and
shift our direction to follow God – the kingdom of
heaven is near indeed. It comes to our very hearts.

Repent from sin. Turn to God. The pivot point at
which Christ's Kingdom comes to our hearts rests
on those two little words.

Gracious Father,
Sometimes we view repentance as something to avoid. Please
help us to see it for the gracious gift that it is, because it brings
us closer to You. Amen.

May 21

Like an Olive Tree

But I am like an olive tree, thriving in the house
of God. I will always trust in God's unfailing love.
I will praise You forever, O God, for what You have done.
I will trust in Your good name in the presence
of Your faithful people.
Psalm 52:8-9

Cultivated in places like South Africa, California, Australia, and the Mediterranean Basin, olive trees are one of the longest-living trees in the world. One olive tree found on the island of Brijuni, Istria is said to be 1,600 years old and still producing fruit.

Olive trees are a picture of prosperity and fruitfulness. In Psalm 52, David observed that although wicked people end in destruction, people who trust in God's unfailing love will thrive and flourish like an olive tree.

The key to a life that flourishes and bears fruit for eternity is found through trusting in God's unfailing love. To trust God is to thrive.

Father,
We want to thrive, too, as we trust in You. Amen.

May 22

Temple Respect

Don't you realize that your body is the temple of the Holy
Spirit, who lives in you and was given to you by God?
You do not belong to yourself, for God bought you with
a high price. So you must honor God with your body.

1 Corinthians 6:19

I have visited some beautiful houses of worship: St. Paul's cathedral in London, St. Stephen's in Vienna, and the cathedral in Koln, Germany. When I entered these buildings, I walked in with a sense of awe. I wouldn't have thought of scratching my name into the stone walls or spray painting a message on them.

No, these houses of worship deserve to be treated with respect. Perhaps we demonstrate more respect for these buildings than we do for our bodies, which are temples in which God lives if we have trusted Christ. Because our bodies were made by God and are inhabited by His Spirit, we need to treat them with the honor God deserves.

Father God,
What a privilege to be Your temple! May we treat it with respect. Amen.

May 23

Multiplication

*Wisdom will multiply your days and add years
to your life. If you become wise, you will be the one
to benefit. If you scorn wisdom, you will be the one to suffer.*
Proverbs 9:11-12

Proverbs is a book of principles that really work. One principle threaded throughout the book is: Wisdom multiplies. Wisdom increases, expands, and produces all kinds of good things in our lives. Wise parents, who raise children with a healthy balance of love and discipline, reap the benefits of well-behaved children (who then often produce well-behaved grandchildren.)

Wise women who practice sexual purity before and during marriage increase the trust factor with their husbands throughout marriage, and all good relationships are built on trust.

Wise people who work hard and plan well in the summer of life usually produce plenty for the winter of life. Simply put, the pursuit of wisdom multiplies our time!

May 24

Generous Father,
Thank You for the rich benefits we experience when we follow Your principles. Amen.

Carried Away

*He will lay both of his hands on the goat's head
and confess over it all the wickedness, rebellion
and sins of the people of Israel. In this way, he will
transfer the people's sins to the head of the goat ... it will
carry all the people's sins upon itself into a desolate land.*

Leviticus 16:21, 22

To find forgiveness of sins in Old Testament days, the high priest would first offer an animal sacrifice for his own sins. Next, he gathered two animals to deal with the people's sins. When the first of the two animals was slaughtered, the curse of sin was passed to the animal instead of on the people who deserved it. The second animal – instead of being slaughtered – was sent into the desert, carrying away the sins of the people.

All of this was a picture of what Jesus would come to do for our sin. God placed the judgment that we deserved onto Jesus, so that we could be forgiven of our sins and made right with God.

Gracious Father,
We're grateful that You provided a way for our sins to be forgiven. Amen.

May 25

Sweet Perfume

But thank God! He has made us His captives and continues to lead us along in Christ's triumphal procession. Now He uses us to spread the knowledge of Christ everywhere, like a sweet perfume.

2 Corinthians 2:14

When I was a child, I loved opening new books and smelling the pages. I still do. It wasn't the scent of a book, though, that caught my attention during a recent visit to a bookstore. While the bookstore clerk totaled up my purchase, I caught a pleasing whiff of something fresh and sweet. "What fragrance are you wearing?" I asked her. "My favorite," she replied. "Mandarin Lily." Because I liked the scent, I ended up purchasing a bottle of the fragrance for myself.

The Bible reminds us that when we walk in close relationship with Christ, our lives – our attitudes, words, and behaviors – will release the sweet evidence of His presence. It's good for us to ponder what kind of whiff those around us are getting.

God,
May the fragrance of Your presence be refreshing to those around us. Amen.

May 26

"But Lord ..."

*"But Lord," Gideon replied, "how can I rescue Israel?
My clan is the weakest in the whole tribe of Manasseh,
and I am the least in my entire family!" The Lord said
to him, "I will be with you. And you will destroy the
Midianites as if you were fighting against one man."*
Judges 6:15-16

We sometimes imagine Bible characters as super-heroes who were larger than life. Most of them had amazing stories; Moses and the Red Sea, Gideon defeating an army of thousands with only 300 men, and Peter walking on water.

But let's not forget that Moses was a shepherd, Gideon was a farmer, and Peter was a fisherman. They were common people who God empowered for His purposes.

If you ever think, "I'm a very common person – I can't do much for God," think again! When God gives us a task, He also give us the strength to accomplish it.

Father,
May we be faithful to You no matter how common the task, remembering that You accomplish big things through common people. Amen.

May 27

Deep and Wide

*And may you have the power to understand, as all
God's people should, how wide, how long, how high,
and how deep His love is. May you experience the love
of Christ, though it is too great to understand fully.*

Ephesians 3:18-19

Give me a choice of where I'd like to vacation, and
I'd choose a place by the ocean. I like watching
things above the water, like waves and jumping
dolphins. I also like thinking about things that live
under the water, like squid and conch shells. After
all, more of the earth is under water than above
water! Covering about 20% of the earth's surface,
the Atlantic Ocean is so large that it's difficult for us
to comprehend.

Maybe that's why the ocean reminds me of God's
love. His love for us is so wide, so long, so high
and so deep that it is too great to fully understand.
That's a great thought for me to ponder whenever I
visit the ocean.

Father,
We long to feel the depth and width of Your love. Amen.

May 28

The Right Direction

Whether the cloud stayed above the Tabernacle for two days, month, or a year, the people of Israel stayed in camp and did not move on. But as soon as it lifted, they broke camp and moved on. So they camped or traveled at the LORD's command.

Numbers 9:22

For the journey God wanted the nation of Israel to make between Mt. Sinai and the land of Canaan, He provided a cloud to guide them. When the cloud moved, the people moved. When the cloud rested, they rested. Even though the Israelites moved at the right times to the right places, there was often a fair amount of discontent and disobedience.

Sometimes, we fall into the same trap. We think more about where and when we're going than about how we're acting in the process.

Is there discontent or disobedience in our hearts today? Before we move any further, it would be good to ask God for His help in living a holy life right where we are today.

Father,
We sometimes think more about logistics than we do about following You. Please forgive us, and help us to please You. Amen.

May 29

Tower over Towers

Let them all praise the name of the Lord.
For His name is very great; His glory towers
over the earth and heaven!

Psalm 148:13

If you were to stand at the top of the Eiffel Tower in Paris (986 ft, 300 m), the Sears Tower in Chicago (1450 ft, 442 m), or the Petronas Towers in Malaysia (1483 ft, 452 m), you would be able to experience the wonder of looking out over surrounding landscapes.

If you were to stand at the bottom of one of these magnificent structures and look up, you might gasp in amazement.

One ancient tower was designed to do just that – the Tower of Babel. But God wasn't pleased, because its arrogant builders had forgotten Him, seeking glory for themselves. God wants us to remember that only He is worthy of our true praise. Earthly buildings may be great, but His glory towers over all of them.

Lord,
We praise You that You are greater than our wildest imaginations. Help us to live in that reality day by day. Amen.

May 30

God Values You

"And the very hairs on your head are all numbered.
So don't be afraid; you are more valuable to God
than a whole flock of sparrows."
Matthew 10:30-31

One of the unspoken questions we human beings
ponder is, *How much worth do I have to those around*
me? Whether we're relating to family, friends,
or co-workers, all of us want to feel valued. If we
were to base our value only on how people treat
us, good treatment would leave us feeling great,
poor treatment would leave us feeling insecure.
That would be an unsettling way to live.

How gracious of God to remind us that He cares
about us so much that He even knows the number
of hairs on our heads. Whether we have more or
less than the average 100,000 hairs on our head, we
are precious to God!

God,
We appreciate reminders in Your Word that we are valuable
to You. Amen.

May 31

June

Strong Refuge

The LORD is good, a strong refuge when trouble comes.
He is close to those who trust in Him.
Nahum 1:7

Troubles in our lives come in many different forms. Whether through anxiety, heartache, pain, or stress – trouble is a matter of when, not if. When we're tired of trouble, we might wonder, *If God really was good, this wouldn't be happening.*

At such times, it's good for us to ponder the little word *when*, mentioned in the verse above. God is good even though trouble comes. God is good at the same time trouble comes. God is good while trouble happens. So how do we experience His goodness in the midst of trouble? By trusting. He is close to those who trust in Him.

Father,
When trouble comes, may we flee to You! Amen.

June 1

Heart's Unrest

*Our actions will show that we belong to the truth,
so we will be confident when we stand before God.
Even if we feel guilty, God is greater than our feelings,
and He knows everything.*

1 John 3:19-20

"Thou hast made us for Thyself, O Lord, and our hearts are restless until they find their rest in Thee." These are the words of Saint Augustine who, in his early years, immersed himself in sensual pleasure. His spiritual autobiography, *The Confessions*, set in the 4th and 5th century A. D., tells of his restlessness and of his heart that continually "condemned" him. But God was pursuing Augustine, and his restless heart gradually drew him to the only One that would set it at rest – Jesus Christ.

In whatever way our lives reflect the restlessness of our hearts, we have the confidence that God is greater than our feelings. When we look to Him for our redemption and help, He is faithful to offer us His rest.

Lord,
May I turn to You as the source of my life's rest and peace.
Amen.

June 2

In His Arms

He will feed His flock like a shepherd. He will carry the lambs
in His arms, holding them close to His heart.
He will gently lead the mother sheep with their young.

Isaiah 40:11

Shepherding is an ancient profession dating back thousands of years. The role of a shepherd is to keep the flock together, protect it from predators, and see that it moves to new pastures as needed. In addition, the shepherd attends to milking the sheep, assisting with the birthing, and shearing the wool.

Jesus called Himself the Good Shepherd, fulfilling the Old Testament theme of God as the Shepherd of His people.

Like sheep, we have an inherent need for safety, care and provision. But our Good Shepherd longs for something beyond the mere duties of shepherding. Jesus longs for relationship – to hold us close to His heart as we turn to Him.

Lord,
When I face the uncertainty of life, I sometimes forget that You
are with me like a Shepherd with His lambs. Help me to rest in
Your loving arms. Amen.

June 3

When I am Afraid

But when I am afraid, I will put my trust in You.
I praise God for what He has promised.
I trust in God, so why should I be afraid?
What can mere mortals do to me?

Psalm 56:3-4

If you were to take a poll of people on a street corner in London asking, "What do you do when you're afraid?" you might hear responses like "worry", "sleep a lot", "shop", or "eat comfort food".

The Old Testament psalmist, David, had the healthiest of responses. He said that when he was afraid, he put his trust in God. I appreciate his honesty – he didn't say, "Because I trust in God I'm never afraid." He said, "When I am afraid, I put my trust in You." His trust was reinforced by praising God for His promises. Rehearsing God's promises reminded David that no one here on earth could ever rob him of eternal life, and that is the ultimate antidote to fear.

Father,
We're grateful that You haven't left us alone to deal with our fears. May we trust in You. Amen.

June 4

Take a Nap

For all who have entered into God's rest have rested from
their labors, just as God did after creating the world.
So let us do our best to enter that rest.

Hebrews 4:10-11

My husband is a napper. Give him ten or fifteen minutes and a place to stretch out, and he can be asleep in seconds. Rest is fundamental to all creation. We rest because God designed life to be so. Following six days of creation, God blessed rest. Rest is so important to God that from Genesis to Revelation He tells His people they must rest one day in seven as an everlasting principle.

In our busy world, we are tempted to squeeze more and more tasks into our week. But when we take the time to follow God's command, we're reminded of a final rest – the rest we will share forever with God our Father.

Father God,
Give me wisdom to plan rest into my week, even as You did. Help me to trust that I will accomplish all that I need to do in the other six days. Amen.

June 5

In His Hands

For the Lord is a great God, a great King above all gods.
He holds in His hands the depths of the earth and the
mightiest mountains. The sea belongs to Him,
for He made it. His hands formed the dry land, too.
Psalm 95:3-5

Recently, I was intrigued by a news headline I read: 20 new ocean species found in Indonesia. The news article reported that before a 2001-2006 survey of catches from local fish markets in Indonesia, there had been gaps in researchers' knowledge of sharks and rays from the region.

Apparently, there are more kinds of sharks and rays in the ocean than was previously realized. Now scientists are aware of new discoveries like the Jimbaran Shovelnose Ray and the Bali Catshark. I smiled when I read the article, remembering the words of Psalm 95 – "The sea belongs to God." The discovery that seemed new to scientists wasn't new to God.

Father God,
We're relieved to know that You've got the whole world in Your hands. Amen.

June 6

Heat Refines

So be truly glad! There is wonderful joy ahead, even
though you have to endure many trials for a little while.
These trials will show that your faith is genuine. It is
being tested as fire tests and purifies gold – though
your faith is far more precious than mere gold.
1 Peter 1:6-7

Are you feeling the heat of trials in your life and wondering how anything good could possibly come from them? Heat hurts. It feels unbearable to us, and our first instinct is to do whatever it takes to get rid of it. When we reflect – years later – on a painful time in our lives, though, we sometimes acknowledge that as difficult as it was, the heat was actually helpful.

Just as gold is heated, causing impurities to rise to the top where they can be skimmed off, the heat of trials in our lives can serve to refine and strengthen us. When we trust God in the fire, we grow to understand that although heat causes pain, heat also causes things to shine.

Father,
May the assurance of joy in the future keep us trusting You today. Amen.

June 7

Words of Comfort

*"You have comforted me by speaking so kindly to me,
even though I am not one of your workers."*
Ruth 2:13

Ruth – an Old Testament woman who was widowed
when she was still young – would have had several
reasons to feel discouraged. Widowed, relocated to
a different country, and destitute, some women in
Ruth's situation might have felt like staying home
permanently and crying. I assume that Ruth had
her moments of grief, but she resolved not to be
paralyzed by them.

An Old Testament law specified that during
harvest time in Israel, harvesters were to leave some
grain in their fields for people like Ruth – people
who were needy or destitute.

God offered comfort to Ruth not only in helping her find grain, but also through the kind words
of the harvester, Boaz. In God's providence, Boaz
ended up being her new husband!

Father,
We know that only You can comfort perfectly, but we'd like to
reflect Your comfort to those who need it. Amen.

June 8

Concern for Others

*"I hate all your show and pretense – the hypocrisy
of your religious festivals and solemn assemblies.
Away with your noisy hymns of praise! I will not listen
to the music of your harps. Instead, I want to see a
mighty flood of justice, an endless river of righteous living."*

Amos 5:21, 23-24

In the Old Testament, God asked the children of Israel to celebrate certain festivals and assemblies – so why was He complaining about their celebrations and noisy hymns? He complained because something had gone terribly wrong. The celebrations had become shams. Underneath the peoples' pretense were selfishness and immorality.

What God intended was for His children to look out for people who didn't have money or influence, but His people were looking out only for themselves. Today, we can fall into the same trap. God doesn't want an outward show of religion. He wants us to live with integrity and goodness, reaching out to needy people. After all, that's how He treats us.

Gracious God,
We're sorry for times we have looked out only for ourselves.
Help us to look out for others. Amen.

June 9

Reconciled

And all of this is a gift from God, who brought us
back to Himself through Christ. And God has given
us this task of reconciling people to Him. For God was
in Christ, reconciling the world to Himself, no longer
counting people's sins against them.
2 Corinthians 5:18-19

In order for us to have a relationship with our
righteous, Holy God, something has to happen.
Before we are able to live different kinds of lives,
Someone needs to settle the account and make
peace on our behalf. Otherwise, we continue to bear
the disgrace and dishonor of our sin.

Yet something *has* happened. When Jesus died
on the cross and took our sins upon Him, He made
it possible for us to become God's friends instead of
being God's enemies.

When we humbly accept God's huge gift in faith,
He transfers Jesus' righteousness over to our account,
and we are reconciled to God. Reconciliation isn't
just for bank statements. Reconciliation is for life.

Father,
We're grateful that Jesus' death made it possible for us to be at
peace with You. Amen.

June 10

Sweeter than Honey

How sweet Your words taste to me,
they are sweeter than honey.
Psalm 119:103

While Benjamin Franklin, American statesman and inventor, was serving at the French Court, he overheard some of the French nobility criticizing the Bible. Having been taught since childhood that the Bible was excellent literature, Benjamin decided to play a trick on them. In longhand, he wrote out the Old Testament book of Ruth, changing every proper name to a French name. Mr. Franklin proceeded to read the book – with his revisions! – to the French aristocrats, who delighted in the story. When they inquired where Benjamin had found this gem of literature, he replied, "It comes from that Book you so despise – *La Sainte Bible!*"

A short book of four chapters that takes only minutes to read, the Old Testament book of Ruth is a sweet rendering of God's incredible grace.

Gracious Father,
We want to savor the sweetness of Your Word. Amen.

June 11

Necessary for Growth

"The rain and snow come down from the heavens and stay on the ground to water the earth. They cause the grain to grow, producing seed for the farmer and bread for the hungry. It is the same with My word. I send it out, and it always produces fruit. It will accomplish all I want it to, and it will prosper everywhere I send it."

Isaiah 55:10-11

The flowers in my yard looked bedraggled and needed a drink. *I'll water them tomorrow*, I thought. How grateful I was to wake up the next morning and hear rain falling. Some people in the world greet rain with absolute euphoria. In Botswana, Africa, the word for rain is also the word for their national currency – 'Pula.' This nation recognizes how important rain is to their economy. For them, rain and money seem a lot alike.

Isn't it curious that the prophet Isaiah likened God's Word to rain as well? God sends out His Word, and it always produces fruit. Just as rain is important to the economy of Botswana, God's Word is necessary for the growth of our hearts.

God,
We need Your Word as much as soil needs rain. Amen.

June 12

Gone Forever

He will wipe every tear from their eyes,
and there will be no more death or sorrow or crying
or pain. All these things are gone forever.
Revelation 21:4

When I was a child, I often wondered what it would be like to be an adult. There were things that I hoped I wouldn't have to do anymore, like riding in the backseat of the car, eating peas, or taking math tests. Now that I'm an adult, I'm relieved that I no longer have to contend with those things.

There are still things that I long to be free from, though, like tears, sorrow, crying, pain, and death. I look forward to a time when they will be gone forever. What a welcome relief that will be. And who knows – since I'll have a new body in heaven, maybe I'll even like peas!

Father,
We're grateful to know that in heaven, there are some things that will be gone forever. Amen.

June 13

Meaning and Purpose

*"Everything is meaningless," says the Teacher,
"completely meaningless!" What do people get
for all their hard work under the sun? Generations
come and generations go, but the earth never changes.*

Ecclesiastes 1:2-4

These words sound bleak to us, but at times they ring true. Like the sun rising and setting day after day, we sometimes wonder where all this activity leads.

"The Teacher" was more in touch than many of us. In his wisdom he could see the hopeless weariness of the generations. Nearly 1,000 years later, the greatest Teacher – Jesus Christ – provided a counterpoint to his predecessor's observations. He said, "I have come that they may have life, and have it to the full." His wisdom and knowledge are complete, and He longs to bring meaning and purpose to each of our lives.

Lord,
Help me not to be overwhelmed by my duties or mindless in my thoughts. Please fill me with the joy and meaning that Your presence and purpose bring to my life. Amen.

June 14

Prosper and Succeed

"Study this Book of Instruction continually. Meditate on it day and night so you will be sure to obey everything written in it. Only then will you prosper and succeed in all you do."
Joshua 1:8

If you want your life to accomplish something – if you'd like to thrive – consider God's words to the Old Testament character, Joshua. From the outset of Joshua's leadership experience, God set forth a plan. In order for Joshua to be successful in his life, he would need to (1) study God's Word (2) continually meditate on it day and night.

God's plan for Joshua is a good plan for us too. Reading God's Word early in the morning helps us prepare for the day. Reading it at night helps us put the day into proper perspective. Day in, day out, we are to read God's Word and think about it deeply. That's the key to a flourishing life!

God,
Your Word is rich. May we spend time in it often. Amen.

God at Work

For God is working in you, giving you the desire
and the power to do what pleases Him.

Philippians 2:13

Do you sometimes feel discouraged because you'd like to please God, but somehow your best efforts to do so seem to get waylaid or sabotaged? When we feel that way, it's helpful for us to remember our source of energy. If we begin with our own efforts and continue to work harder and harder ... we'll often run out of energy.

God has given us a better way of approaching life. When we trust in Christ, God's Spirit inhabits our hearts. With His presence, He brings His energy to work in our hearts, giving us both the desire and the power to please Him. Acknowledging God's power, submitting to God's power, and stepping out in God's power = His energy in us.

Father,
We're grateful that You provide the desire and the power in us to please You. Amen.

June 16

Morning, Noon, and Night

But I will call on God, and the LORD will rescue me.
Morning, noon, and night I cry out in my distress,
and the LORD hears my voice.

Psalm 55:16-17

There are many kinds of pain in the world. One of the worst kinds is to be deceived or betrayed by someone close to us. Feelings of sadness and anger can be so intense that – initially – it's difficult to go for ten minutes without feeling the pain.

David, the psalmist, knew what that was like. It's helpful and even encouraging that he wrote out his feelings, because his feelings often seem to validate ours. David said that his heart pounded, his body trembled, and he wished that he could fly away. At his lowest moment, he even wished bad things on his enemy. But where did David land? He had confidence that God would hear him, and he called on God – morning, noon, and night. We can, too.

Father,
We're grateful that we can call out to You. Thank You that You hear us and help us. Amen.

June 17

Godliness and Contentment

*Yet true godliness with contentment is itself great wealth.
After all, we brought nothing with us when we came into the
world, and we can't take anything with us when we leave it.
So if we have enough food and clothing, let us be content.*

1 Timothy 6:6-8

In these few verses, Paul taught Timothy how to realize a rich and fulfilling life; pursue godliness and contentment. A person who is godly lives a holy, God-honoring life through the power of God's Spirit. A person who is content is satisfied, peaceful, fulfilled, and at ease. Paul also pointed out to Timothy how *not* to pursue a rich and fulfilling life – by being concerned merely with the pursuit of things.

One of my favorite pastors, Kent Hughes, said, "Have you ever seen a funeral hearse pulling a trailer?" We may accumulate riches when we're alive, but when we depart, it's only the riches of our souls that we will take with us. There's great wealth in godliness and contentment.

Father,
Please help us as we seek to pursue the right things. Amen.

Cedars of Lebanon

*So I am planning to build a Temple to honor
the name of the L**ORD** my God, just as He had
instructed my father, David. Therefore, please
command that cedars from Lebanon be cut for me.*
1 Kings 5:5-6

The cedar trees of Lebanon are particularly significant in Middle Eastern culture. The Egyptians, Assyrians, and Babylonians exploited this timber that was prized for its length, strength, and fragrance. Solomon requested cedar from Lebanon to be cut so he could use it to build God's Temple.

Nebuchadnezzar, the Babylonian ruler, boasted in an inscription, "I brought for building, mighty cedars, which I cut down with my pure hands on Mount Lebanon." Solomon and Nebuchadnezzar both treasured the resource of cedar trees, but Solomon used the wood to build God's Temple while Nebuchadnezzar was the one who destroyed it.

God wants us to honor Him with the things He's created – are we doing that?

Lord,
Help me to honor Your name with the resources You have provided for me. Amen.

June 19

On the Fringe

A woman who had suffered for twelve years
with constant bleeding came up behind Him.
She touched the fringe of His robe, for she thought,
"If I can just touch His robe, I will be healed."
Jesus turned around, and when He saw her He said,
"Daughter, be encouraged! Your faith has made you well."

Matthew 9:20-22

A sick woman who had lived for twelve years on the outskirts of society suddenly became the focus of Jesus' attention. This was probably a huge surprise to her. Hoping not to be noticed in the crowd, the woman came up behind Jesus, reached out, and touched the fringe of His robe. I'm sure she didn't expect what happened next. Jesus turned around, looked at her, healed her, spoke to her, and encouraged her. He did all that for a woman who, by society's standards, was a nobody.

Do you ever feel as though you or someone you know is living on the fringe and no one seems to care? Remember, Jesus cares about everyone.

Father,
We're grateful that we are not on the fringe with You. Please help us to treat others the same way. Amen.

June 20

Healing and Hope

*"Make a replica of a poisonous snake and attach it to a pole.
All who are bitten will live if they simply look at it!"*
Numbers 21:8
*"As Moses lifted up the bronze snake on a pole in the
wilderness, so the Son of Man must be lifted up so that
everyone who believes in Him will have eternal life."*
John 3:14-15

The picture of a snake wrapped around a pole is
a picture of both horror and hope. Horror, because
after the children of Israel complained in the desert
they were bitten by venomous snakes and were
about to die. Hope, because Moses put a symbolic
snake up on a pole and told the people that anyone
who looked at the snake would live.

The snake symbolizes our sin, since it was a
serpent that tempted Adam and Eve, bringing sin
into the world. The pole symbolizes the cross, where
Jesus took our sins upon Himself in order to save
us from sin and death. Simple faith in Christ brings
healing and hope – here on earth and forever.

Father,
Thank You for providing healing and hope through Jesus.
Amen.

June 21

A Prize Ahead

I have fought the good fight, I have finished the race,
and I have remained faithful. And now the prize
awaits me. And the prize is not just for me but for
all who eagerly look forward to His appearing.
2 Timothy 4:7-8

What kinds of prizes have you received in your lifetime? Candy for winning a game of bingo? A week at summer camp for memorizing a chapter of the Bible? A bonus check for a good job at work? All of us like to be rewarded for a job well-done. We like the idea of a prize that's waiting for us around the corner.

However, in the hustle and bustle of our busy lives here on earth, we sometimes forget the magnitude of the gift of eternal life that is waiting for us in heaven. Candy melts in our mouths. Summer camp comes to an end. A financial bonus gets spent on college or a vacation. But the prize of eternal life never ends.

Father,
May we remain faithful to You until the day we see You face to face. Amen.

June 22

True and Right

End the evil of those who are wicked,
and defend the righteous. For You look deep within
the mind and heart, O righteous God. God is my shield,
saving those whose hearts are true and right.

Psalm 7:9-10

More than once, I've lost a pocketknife while going through an airport security check. It's easy to forget about a pocketknife stored in a purse or a pocket, but scanning machines are quick to uncover such things.

Like implements that are stashed away in a purse or a bag, our minds and hearts contain thoughts, words and attitudes that are also hidden from sight. They aren't hidden to God, though. That reality can be frightening and comforting – frightening if we're trying to hide, and comforting if we're longing for God's help.

When we desire hearts that are true and right, we need not fear coming to God. We find Him to be the God who saves us, protects us, and defends us.

Father,
We long for hearts that are true and right before You. Amen.

June 23

Prayer Bowls

*And when He took the scroll, the four living beings and
the twenty-four elders fell down before the Lamb.
Each one had a harp, and they held gold bowls filled
with incense, which are the prayers of God's people.*

Revelation 5:8

Have you ever entered a sweepstakes competition
and thought, *Well, I filled out the form, but that's the
last I'll ever see of that! Surely nothing more will come of
this.* Even though thousands of people might enter
a sweepstakes, the only entry that really matters is
the one that wins.

Have you ever prayed to God and wondered
if your prayers made it past the ceiling? According to Revelation 5:8, they do. There we learn that
the prayers of God's people are like sweet incense
collected in gold bowls. Not only are our prayers
heard by God, but they're collected. The prayers of
God's people make a difference!

Father,
Thank You that our prayers aren't tossed aside, but that they
are important to You. Amen.

June 24

Hidden Treasures

Tune your ears to wisdom, and concentrate on understanding. Cry out for insight, and ask for understanding. Search for them as you would for silver; seek them like hidden treasures. Then you will understand what it means to fear the Lord, and you will gain knowledge of God.

Proverbs 2:2-5

Since the Bible encourages us to search for wisdom and understanding as we would search for silver, the question that comes to mind is, "How would we search for silver?" If we went straight to the source, we might visit silver mines in Australia, Canada, Mexico, South America, or Nevada. At those locations, we'd find silver that is used all around the world for coins, jewelry, photography, and musical instruments, among other things.

Thankfully, a search for wisdom and understanding doesn't require expensive travel to other countries. Like anything of value, it requires time and effort. We begin by searching in ... the Bible.

Father,
As we 'mine' Your Word, it's a privilege to get to know You better. Amen.

June 25

A Dose of Cheer

A cheerful heart is good medicine,
but a broken spirit saps a person's strength.
Proverbs 17:22

Whether it comes in the form of an antibiotic, anesthetic, or antiseptic, medicine helps to alleviate, cure, or prevent some of our illnesses. Medicine can be costly, though. Some of the tablets and tonics available on the market today cost as much money as it costs to feed one family for a month.

How refreshing, then, to learn that a cheerful heart – something that costs no money – is considered good medicine. So where do we go to acquire a cheerful heart? Psalm 94:18-19 points us in the right direction, "I cried out, 'I am slipping!' Your unfailing love, O LORD, supported me. When doubts filled my mind, Your comfort gave me renewed hope and cheer." Through God's Word and God's Spirit, we can receive comfort that produces cheer. Ask God for a large dose of it today.

Father,
Please replace our doubting hearts with Your love, Your comfort and Your cheer. Amen.

June 26

Detours

*For the next two years, Paul lived in Rome
at his own expense. He welcomed all
who visited him, boldly proclaiming the
Kingdom of God and teaching about the
Lord Jesus Christ. And no one tried to stop him.*
Acts 28:30-31

Under house arrest in Rome for two years, the Apostle Paul was confined, but not confused. If that had happened to me, I might have felt disoriented and flustered, thinking, *God, this isn't the way I thought things were meant to turn out. I was anxious to travel around the world serving You, and here I am stuck in a house for two years!*

How did Paul handle the detour? Not with confusion, anger, or self-pity. Instead, he chose to be hospitable to anyone who visited him, talking about God's Kingdom and teaching about Jesus. Sure, detours can be discouraging; but detours can also be opportunities to display God's truth, grace, and power.

Father,
When we're faced with detours in our experiences, please help us to trust that You are working out Your good plans. Amen.

June 27

Lasting Confidence

*"Blessed are those who trust in the L*ORD *and have made the L*ORD *their hope and confidence. They are like trees planted along a riverbank."*
Jeremiah 1:7-8
The hope of the godless evaporate. Their confidence hangs by a thread. They are leaning on a spider's web.
Job 8:13-14

As impressive and intricate as a spider's web is, it isn't exactly permanent. Spun out of silk by an eight-legged arachnid, a web is often eaten and rebuilt by its industrious spider each morning!

The Bible likens the transient nature of a spider web to the hopes of the godless – pointing out that their confidence hangs only by a thread. A more promising picture is painted of the person who places hope in God. She will not only be blessed, but she is likened to a healthy, stable and productive tree planted along a riverbank. When we place our hope in God, we experience the lasting blessings of confidence and security.

Father,
We're grateful that trusting You brings lasting hope. Amen.

June 28

Time with Jesus

*When they climbed back into the boat,
the wind stopped. Then the disciples worshiped Him.
"You really are the Son of God!" they exclaimed.*

Matthew 14:32-33

The first time Jesus calmed a storm, His disciples responded, "Who is this man? Even the winds and waves obey Him!" (Matt. 8:23-27). The second time the disciples watched Jesus calm a storm, their faith seemed to have grown. The Bible records that they worshiped Jesus and exclaimed, "You really are the Son of God!"

The more time the disciples spent with Jesus – particularly the challenging times – the better they understood who He was. Isn't that true of all of us? It's often during the stormy times of life – when all the props seem to be pulled out from under us – that we discover who God is, how powerful He is, and how much He cares about us.

Father,
We're grateful for accounts in Your Word that demonstrate how much You care about us. Amen.

June 29

The King's Garden

*Then the L*ORD *God planted a garden in Eden in the east, and there He placed the man He had made. The L*ORD *God made all sorts of trees grow up from the ground ... Then God looked over all He had made, and He saw that it was very good.*
Genesis 2:8-9, 1:31

If you're ever in London, consider visiting Regent's Park. The park is home to one of England's finest rose collections – Queen Mary's garden. Strolling through the garden on a bright, sunny day is an enthralling experience. What creativity the designers displayed as they planned colors, variety, and layout!

The beauty of this garden hints at the beauty of the King of king's original garden – Eden. What a spectacular place it must have been! All the beauty in the world reminds us of the infinite creativity of our creator King, the Lord God. It is a mere shadow of His extravagant splendor. And to think that He shares that beauty with us!

Lord,
You have made all things to bring honor to Yourself. Give me eyes to see Your beauty in the sight and fragrance of a single rose. Amen.

June 30

July

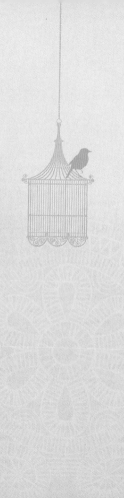

New Confidence

And because we are His children, God has sent the Spirit of His Son into our hearts, prompting us to call out, "Abba, Father." Now you are no longer a slave but God's own child. And since you are His child, God has made you His heir.

Galatians 4:6-7

While cleaning out his parents' attic one summer's day, a fourteen-year-old cross-country runner found a box of medals and ribbons that his father had won while he was a runner at Purdue University.

Up until that point, the boy hadn't even known that his father had been a champion runner. But badges that mattered to the father in the past now mattered to the son. In a curious way, the son gained new confidence in his running. When we become God's children through faith in Christ, we gain a similar type of confidence. We find new worth based on what Christ's death and resurrection have accomplished for us. We begin to have new desires. Things that matter to God now matter to us.

Father,
Thank You for the security and confidence we gain because of being Your children. Amen.

July 1

Hopeful News

All of us, like sheep, have strayed away.
We have left God's paths to follow our own.
Yet the LORD laid on Him the sins of us all.

Isaiah 53:6

Back in 1976, Thomas Harris wrote a book touting the message, "I'm OK, You're OK." In 700 B. C., the Old Testament prophet Isaiah wrote a book proclaiming the message, "I'm a needy person, you're a needy person."

The stark reality is that we are a needy, sinful bunch, and that's why we need a Savior. Contrary to what some people think, this is not hopeless news. This is hopeful news. We have a sin problem, and Jesus, the sinless Son of God, is the One who can help us.

He died on the cross for our sins, making it possible for us to be forgiven and to inherit God's righteousness and Spirit. Jesus was wounded so that we could be healed.

Father,
We're grateful that You made a way for our sins to be forgiven.
Thank You for sending Jesus to be our Savior. Amen.

July 2

Everything We Need

"So don't worry about these things, saying what will we eat? What will we drink? What will we wear? These things dominate the thoughts of unbelievers, but your heavenly Father already knows all your needs.
Seek the Kingdom of God above all else and live righteously, and He will give you everything you need."
Matthew 6:31-33

It's easy for worries and cares to monopolize our thoughts. Sometimes, we're weighed down with questions like "Will there be enough money for our kids to go to college?" Or, "How will we ever make the house payment this month?" The Bible reminds us that if we let these thoughts control our minds, we're acting like people who don't believe God.

We're not supposed to ignore these kinds of concerns, and it's right to plan ahead and take responsibility in healthy ways. But since God already knows all of our needs, it's wise for us to become consumed with Him instead of being consumed by our needs. As we seek Him and obey Him, He will provide for our needs.

Heavenly Father,
We're grateful that You see and meet our needs. Amen.

July 3

The Key to Life

"Today I have given you the choice between life and death ... Oh that you would choose life, so that you and your descendants might live! You can make this choice by loving the LORD your God, obeying Him, and committing yourself firmly to Him. This is the key to your life."

Deuteronomy 30:19-20

A financial adviser says that the key to experiencing a profitable retirement is to begin early and plan ahead. A fitness consultant says that the key to losing weight is to eat less and exercise more.

We look for keys because we want to know the solution to a problem or the means to accomplish a goal. Moses, who recorded God's Words under the influence of God's Spirit, left us a threefold key to experiencing life, not death – blessings, not curses. Love God, obey God, and commit to God.

As we love Him, obey Him, and commit ourselves to Him, we will experience a fulfilling life. That's the key.

God,
Thank You for blessing us with the discernment to make wise choices. Amen.

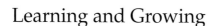

Learning and Growing

*Put on your new nature, and be renewed as you
learn to know your Creator and become like Him.*

Colossians 3:10

My husband just purchased a new cell phone for
me. The phone has many features on it that will
prove to be valuable – *if* I am willing to invest time
to learn about them.

Growing in Christ is like that. When we place
our faith in Christ, God gives us a new nature. In
order to become acquainted with that new nature,
we need to take time to learn about Christ. We can
do that through reading the Bible, praying, and
engaging in Christian community.

Growing in our new nature is a lifelong process
of learning, growth, and renewal. A rich life is
available to each of us if we're willing to take the
time to know Christ better.

Father,
Thank You that the way to grow in Christ is not hidden. Thank
You for Your Word, and Your Spirit who helps us. Amen.

July 5

A Time Like This

*"If you keep quiet at a time like this, deliverance
and relief for the Jews will arise from some other place,
but you and your relatives will die. Who knows if perhaps
you were made queen for just such a time as this?"*
Esther 4:14

A search for King Xerxes' new queen ... beautiful young Esther ... self-serving Haman attempts to kill Esther's cousin, Mordecai ... Esther courageously asks for the king's help ... the king's sleepless night ... the king honors Mordecai ... Esther reveals Haman's wicked plot ... Haman is sentenced to death ... the king appoints Mordecai to a government position ... God preserves the Jewish people. The Old Testament book of Esther showcases God's sovereignty and intervention in human lives. God placed Esther in a position where her life made an incredible difference, saving a whole nation.

As you exercise courage and faith in your corner of the world, how might God use you to make a difference for His Kingdom?

Father,
Like Esther, may we not stay silent when we can speak up for Your truth. Amen.

Before the Rockies

*Lord, through all the generations You have been our home!
Before the mountains were born, before You gave birth to
the earth and the world, from beginning to end, You are
God.*

Psalm 90:1-2

Situated in the heart of Colorado, Rocky Mountain National Park is one of America's great treasures. With peaks rising higher than 14,000 feet, the park contains 450 miles of streams, 150 lakes, and an abundance of wildlife.

The geological age of the park is a subject debated by scientists, but God knows the actual history of this wonder. In His creative power, only He could have conceived of such spectacular beauty and diversity, given to us for pleasure and as an indication of His existence and power.

Before the birth of these mountains, God existed. He is the eternal God from beginning to end.

Lord God,
Thank You for creating such a magnificent world! We're grateful that You are a personal God, and have become our very home by faith in Jesus. Amen.

July 7

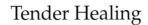

Tender Healing

A man with leprosy came and knelt in front of Jesus, begging to be healed. "If You are willing, You can heal me and make me clean," he said. Moved with compassion, Jesus reached out and touched him. "I am willing," He said. "Be healed!" Instantly the leprosy disappeared, and the man was healed.

Mark 1:40-42

Leprosy disfigured people as it spread, and as a result lepers were banished from their families, friends, and communities. Sin affects us the same way. It spreads easily, deforms our lives, and isolates us from one another.

The beautiful story of how Jesus healed a leper is a tender picture of the healing He offers to us. When the leper knelt before Jesus, Jesus was moved with compassion, touched the leper, and healed him. He didn't just talk – He did something!

We come to God asking for His help. He cares and reaches out, and He offers us forgiveness and healing. Only God can deal with us so powerfully and so tenderly.

Father,
Thank You that we can trust You to deal with us gently. Amen.

July 8

Our Shelter

Keep me safe, O God, for I have come to You for refuge.
Psalm 16:1

Grilled burgers, grape soda, games, and prizes; church picnics were a treasured part of my childhood. The most memorable picnic for me, however, was the year of the thunderstorm.

When the thunderstorm threatened to spoil our fun, everyone present scurried underneath the roof of a large stone rain shelter. There, we were protected from lightning and driving rain. Safe and secure, we laughed and talked until the rain had passed.

My childhood image of a rain shelter that offered safety from a physical storm is not unlike the security and refuge that a relationship with God offers. During storms that threaten the state of our hearts and minds, God is there, waiting for us to flee to Him. He wants to be our shelter of security and refuge.

Father,
Our hearts long for security, but sometimes we look for it in the wrong places. Help us to come to You. Amen.

July 9

The Birth of Time Zones

God set these lights in the sky to light the earth, to govern the day and night, and to separate the light from the darkness. And God saw that it was good.
Genesis 1:17-18

In 1884, delegates from 25 nations met in Washington, D. C. to agree upon an international standard for measuring time. They divided the earth into 24 time zones beginning at the Prime Meridian, which runs through the Royal Greenwich Observatory in Greenwich, England.

The nations agreeing to this standard were only acknowledging and organizing for people what God had created long before the keeping of time. God, who never sleeps, watches over everything in the world 24/7, no matter what time zone we're in.

He organized the "lights" in the sky – the sun, moon and stars, and gave them to us to separate day and night. They stand as evidence of His great creative power and wisdom.

Creator God,
Each time we look up and see the sun and the moon, may we be reminded of Your sovereign wisdom and creativity throughout the universe. Amen.

July 10

Flooded with Light

I pray that your hearts will be flooded with light so that you can understand the confident hope He has given to those He called.

Ephesians 1:18

After Hurricane Andrew's destruction in Florida, it was discovered that an elderly woman, Norena, had lived in her home without power for almost fifteen years! Due to an unscrupulous contractor and an insurance settlement that ran out, Norena decided just to "live with it".

After someone from the neighborhood informed the Miami-Dade Mayor of her plight, a contractor was brought in and Norena quickly found her house "flooded with light." When interviewed by local reporters, Norena said, "It's hard to describe having [power] come on ... It's overwhelming."

When God calls us out of darkness, we are overwhelmed, too. We're overwhelmed with hope, forgiveness of sins, grace, peace, wisdom, and the presence of the Holy Spirit. We're flooded with light!

Father,
Please help us to realize the confidence that Your light brings to our lives. Amen.

July 11

Priorities

Better to spend your time at funerals than at parties.
After all, everyone dies – so the living should take
this to heart. Ecclesiastes 7:2

Imagine that you've been given a choice: you may attend either a funeral service or a festive party. The party would include talking, laughing, and feasting, while the funeral would involve listening, reflecting and mourning. Which would you choose?

Some years ago, I played my violin for funeral services at a nearby funeral home. The gatherings were deeply emotional, whether loved ones were celebrating a life well-lived, grieving their losses, or reflecting on life in general. Each service offered me an opportunity to think about what is most important in life.

Living life with the end in mind is a good way to gain perspective and set priorities. Funerals are better than parties at bringing focus to how we live.

Lord,
You have given each of us an exact number of days to live on this earth. Help us to live them in a way that is pleasing to You. Amen.

July 12

Faithful under Pressure

Daniel, Hananiah, Mishael, and Azariah were four of the young men chosen, all from the tribe of Judah. The chief of staff renamed them with these Babylonian names: Daniel was called Belteshazzar. Hananiah was called Shadrach. Mishael was called Meshach. Azariah was called Abednego. But Daniel was determined not to defile himself.

Daniel 1:6-8

Daniel, Hananiah, Mishael, and Azariah, were only about sixteen when they were taken hostage by King Nebuchadnezzar and deported from Judah to Babylon.

One of the first things Nebuchadnezzar did was change their names. It was an attempt to change their devotion from the true God to Babylonian gods. Because Daniel and his friends had a clear purpose and unwavering faith in God, they didn't give in to the pressures around them.

At first, it appeared that they would lose their lives, but God walked with them and rescued Daniel's friends out of the fiery furnace. A life of faith in God is a triumphant life.

Father,
Give us grace not to give in to pressures around us. Amen.

July 13

Interest in Others

Don't be selfish; don't try to impress others.
Be humble, thinking of others as better than yourselves.
Don't look out only for your own interests.
You must have the same attitude that Christ Jesus had.
Philippians 2:3-5

Hardly a day goes by where I don't struggle with selfishness in one form or another. Whether it's trying to impress one person or ignoring another, I sometimes look out for myself instead of looking out for others.

Christ wants me to have a much different attitude – an unselfish attitude. It's no coincidence that the word *others* is mentioned three times in the verses above. God wants me to follow Christ's example.

Christ came to be our Shepherd and look out for us. Instead of living here on earth with a greedy, what's-in-it-for-me attitude, He cares about us so much that He gave His lifeblood for us. What a humble example.

Father,
I confess my selfishness to You. Please fill me with Your grace so that I will think more of others. Amen.

Plans for Us

The LORD will work out His plans for my life –
for Your faithful love, O LORD, endures forever.
Don't abandon me, for You made me.

Psalm 138:8

Draw a line across a sheet of paper and make a tiny dot somewhere on the line. If the dot represents us and the (infinite!) line represents God's plan for the world, we see that God's designs are much bigger than we sometimes think.

The span of our lives on this earth might seem to be only a short dot on the line, but when we live in relationship with the eternal, faithful God, we become part of a plan that's much bigger than anything we ever imagined.

The faithful Lord of the universe has plans for us! The loving God who made us will never abandon us.

Faithful Father,
Thank You for the assurance that You will never leave us alone.
Amen.

July 15

Let Children Come

"One day some parents brought their children to Jesus
so He could lay His hands on them and pray for them.
But the disciples scolded the parents for bothering Him.
But Jesus said, "Let the children come to Me.
Don't stop them!" Matthew 19:13-14

Boarding a recent sixteen hour flight to Hong Kong, my husband took his assigned seat. To his chagrin, he found that he was surrounded by five families with children under the age of four! For most of the flight, the plane was noisy – it proved to be a patience-building time.

While Jesus' life was filled with constant activity and crowds following Him everywhere He went, He always had time for people – especially those that had little social standing.

Jesus' disciples didn't seem to understand this. They tried to turn the children away, but Jesus would have none of it. He took the children in His arms and blessed them. Jesus elevated the worth of children.

July 16

Lord,
Thank You that in Your love You have never turned away anyone who came to You for mercy or care. Amen.

A Love Story

The LORD says, "Then I will heal you of your faithlessness;
My love will know no bounds, for My anger will be gone
forever. I will be to Israel like a refreshing dew
from heaven."

Hosea 14:4-5

Hosea, an 8th century B. C. prophet, was called by God to a strange life. He was told to marry a promiscuous woman, some of whose children would be born of prostitution.

The story of Hosea's love for his wife, and his persistent actions to redeem her from her unfaithfulness was written to show Israel then – and us today – that God is faithful. Even in our rebellion, God pursues us in His faithfulness.

The book of Hosea also demonstrates how God works in our hearts, healing us from the ways in which we have rejected Him. It is a love story written by Hosea, but it is for us too.

Lord,
Thank You that You willingly heal us of our sin and faithlessness. Thank You that Your love for us is never ending. Amen.

July 17

Lasting Heirloom

So each generation should set its hope anew on God,
not forgetting His glorious miracles and obeying His
commands. Then they will not be like their ancestors –
stubborn, rebellious, and unfaithful, refusing to give
their hearts to God. Psalm 78:7-8

If you are a generation or two ahead of any of your family members, you have an opportunity to pass down a priceless heirloom. If you have children, nieces, nephews or grandchildren, you can pass down the truth and grace of God's Word.

In Psalm 78, God spelled out four specific reasons for sharing His Word with subsequent generations. First, He wants us to set our hope and reliance on Him. Second, He wants us to remember His glorious works. Third, He wants us to be obedient. And fourth, He desires that we learn from the past, because people who don't learn from the past often end up reliving it. We can give the gift of God's Word.

God,
May we share Your Word with young members of our families. Amen.

July 18

Wildfire Words

The tongue is a small thing that makes grand speeches.
But a tiny spark can set a great forest on fire.
And the tongue is a flame of fire. It can set your
whole life on fire, for it is set on fire by hell itself.

James 3:5-6

Wildfires are common in most parts of the world and tend to be started by lightning, volcanic eruptions, or human carelessness. Driven on by winds, dryness, and sheer enormity, wildfires can destroy thousands of acres of land and property, sometimes causing irreparable damage.

James chose the dramatic picture of a wildfire to impress on us the terrible effects our negative words can have on others. Carelessly spoken words can crush a child's spirit, set off a conflict in an organization, or hopelessly alienate a husband and wife.

Words count. Choosing our words carefully today pays huge dividends in our relationships down the road. What effects are our words having on those around us?

Lord,
May Your Spirit guide my words today. May they bring refreshment to others. Amen.

July 19

In God's Hands

But I am trusting You, O LORD, saying, "You are my God!" My future is in Your hands ... Let Your favor shine on Your servant. In Your unfailing love, rescue me. Don't let me be disgraced, O LORD, for I call out to You for help.

Psalm 31:14-17

Sometimes we live as though our future is in our hands – or in the hands of our stockbroker, our boss, or our healthcare network. But the Bible explains that everything that happens to us is in God's hands.

Since we have observed God to be righteous, faithful, and loving to others in the past, we can trust that He is working out His good plan for our lives, too – even in the midst of painful or difficult circumstances.

Seeing what God has done in the past, we are prompted to believe that He will help us too. And as we wait, it's comforting to know that we're not the only ones who have struggled with waiting.

Father,
It's reassuring to read accounts of others who struggled with waiting. We're encouraged that they found You to be faithful. Amen.

Faith, Not Perfection

*You received the Spirit because you believed the
message you heard about Christ ... After starting
your Christian lives in the Spirit, why are you now
trying to become perfect by your own human effort?*
Galatians 3:3-4

A chef strives to bake the perfect cake ... A hairstylist
aims for the perfect haircut ... A pianist dreams of
playing a perfect performance. Have you ever felt
pressure – from inside or outside yourself – to live
perfectly?

The apostle Paul saw that Christian believers
were struggling for perfection through their own
efforts, and he felt compelled to give them a reality
check. He reminded them that they became God's
children solely on the basis of their faith in Christ.

That was how they began, and that was how
they were to continue living. Faith in Christ is more
than just the introduction to the Christian life – it's
the whole story!

God,
Instead of striving for perfection that's impossible to attain, we
want to depend on Your Spirit. Amen.

July 21

Benefits of Wisdom

She [wisdom] offers you long life in her right hand,
and riches and honor in her left. She will guide
you down delightful paths; all her ways are satisfying.
Wisdom is a tree of life to those who embrace her;
happy are those who hold her tightly.

Proverbs 3:16-18

If we read this verse for the first time, we might think that anyone who chooses to pursue wisdom would be guaranteed a long life, riches, and honor. Maybe that could happen in a perfect world – but that's not what we were born into.

It's helpful, then, to remember that the book of Proverbs is brimming with principles – not promises. Warren Wiersbe reminds us that "Proverbs are generalizations about life and not promises for us to claim."

If we choose to welcome wisdom and work at incorporating it into our lives, we won't necessarily be assured of an easy life. But we can be certain that our lives won't be wasted. They will be meaningful, and we will be blessed.

Father,
We are grateful for the varied benefits of Your wisdom. Amen.

July 22

Creative Service

Then the LORD said to Moses, "Look, I have specifically chosen Bezalel son of Uri, grandson of Hur, of the tribe of Judah. I have filled him with the Spirit of God, giving him great wisdom, ability, and expertise in all kinds of crafts."

Exodus 31:1-3

God equipped Bezalel with all the gifts necessary to build the tabernacle and the ark of the covenant, and He continues to equip His servants today.

My friend Marge is one example. While Marge's husband, Richard, has performed eye surgery in needy parts of the world, Marge – a gifted artist – has drawn murals in those same locations: Noah's ark for a pediatric hospital in India, and Jesus healing the blind man in a hospital in Mongolia. Each of these murals tells a story of God's power – without using words.

God's Good News is still spreading around the world through the gifts He gives to His people. Along with the abilities God gives, He also provides strength for each task.

Master Creator,
Open our eyes to the variety of ways that we can serve You.
Amen.

July 23

Inside Out

*"But the words you speak come from the heart –
that's what defiles you. For from the heart
come evil thoughts. These are what defile you."*
Matthew 15:18-20

Opening the door to a room in our finished basement, I smelled something musty. *That's funny,* I thought. *Everything looks fine.* Pulling back the carpet, I discovered that water was seeping in from outside our house.

My husband and I eventually learned that in order to repair a crack on the outside of the house, we had to knock out part of the inside wall first. Matters of the heart often work the same way. What's going on inside our hearts usually manifests itself in our words.

When our words give off offensive and musty odors, our hearts need to be transformed by Christ. When we turn to Him in repentance and dependence, He is faithful to freshen things up, changing things from the inside out.

Father,
We bring our hearts to You, thankful that Your Spirit changes us. Amen.

July 24

God's Presence

*Then Moses said, "If You don't personally go with us,
don't make us leave this place. How will anyone know that
You look favorably on me – on me and Your people –
if You don't go with us? For Your presence among us
sets Your people and me apart from all other people on the
earth."*

Exodus 33:15-16

*Things don't look good for me or for the honor of Your
name, God.* I wonder if Moses felt that way. He told
God that he couldn't go any further unless he knew
that God would go with him.

If God didn't go with him and the Israelites,
Moses reasoned, their reputation would be doomed,
and so would God's. How did God respond? He
promised that He would do as Moses had asked
and would look favorably on him. He also said that
He knew Moses by name and that He would show
Moses His glory.

When things in life don't make sense, ask God
for His presence. Safety isn't the absence of danger.
Safety is the presence of God.

Father,
When things in our lives don't make sense, may we look to You
for assurances of Your presence. Amen.

July 25

Full of Flavor

"You are the salt of the earth. But what good is salt if it has lost its flavor? Can you make it salty again? It will be thrown out and trampled underfoot as worthless."

Matthew 5:13

I recently ate an ear of corn without sprinkling salt on it. It tasted ... blah. Without salt, some foods seem disappointing – corn on the cob, scrambled eggs, and mashed potatoes with gravy, to be specific. Sprinkle a little salt over these foods, though, and they smack with flavor.

Just as table salt brings zest to some of our favorite foods, Christ's presence causes us to stand out to people around us.

If we follow Christ closely, our lives can affect others as positively as salt flavors food. We will be zesty, not blah. The closer we get to the Source, the saltier we will be.

Father,
We want to remain faithful to You and retain our saltiness.
Amen.

July 26

Life-Giving Words

The words of the godly are a life-giving fountain;
the words of the wicked conceal violent intentions.

Proverbs 10:11

Located in Geneva, Switzerland, the Jet d'Eau is one of the largest fountains in the world. Whenever the fountain is operating, the water sails up into the air, reaching about 140 meters.

The writer of Proverbs compares the words of a godly person to a life-giving fountain – a fitting picture to ponder. As we are connected to God, the Source of all life, we can speak words that will edify, comfort, and counsel those around us.

The reverse is also true. If we spew out destructive words, we can hurt people. It all depends on the source that we're drawing from. As we gain wisdom from time spent in God's Word and ask for His help, our words can have a life-giving effect.

God,
We want our words to be life-giving to all we come in contact with. Amen.

July 27

Beyond Our Power

Then Pharaoh said to Joseph, "I had a dream last night, and no one here can tell me what it means. But I have heard that when you hear about a dream you can interpret it." "It is beyond my power to do this," Joseph replied. "But God can tell you what it means and set you at ease." Genesis 41:15-16

On occasions when we show kindness to a friend or help a family member in need, we sometimes receive thanks and a compliment. It is nice to be acknowledged and a simple 'Thank you' is always appreciated.

There are times, though, when it's good to go a step further. When we know that a helpful thing we have said or done was clearly a consequence of God's grace or power, it is God-honoring to acknowledge His help to those around us.

As we are helped, comforted, and strengthened by God's Spirit, it's good for us to share that with other people.

God,
I'm warmed by Joseph's humble example. He didn't take credit for himself, but acknowledged You. I want to do that, too. Amen.

July 28

Pray Often

*God knows how often I pray for you. Day and night I bring
you and your needs in prayer to God, whom I serve with
all my heart by spreading the Good News about His Son.*
Romans 1:9

How often do you eat? How often do you collect
your mail? Things we do often are things we do
frequently, regularly, again and again. We tend to
make time for things that are important to us – like
eating and hobbies.

Prayer is more than important – it's our lifeline.
Paul, a New Testament apostle, prayed day and
night. Daniel, an Old Testament prophet, prayed
three times a day. Prayer was their source of wisdom, guidance, and strength – things that each of
us need daily.

Prayer doesn't cost money, we don't need to
make an appointment, and there are no limits to
how much we can pray. We can start early and pray
often.

God,
To know that someone cares about us enough to pray for us
touches us deeply. May we show the same care for others.
Amen.

July 29

God's Honor

*Help us, O God of our salvation! Help us for the
glory of Your name. Save us and forgive
our sins for the honor of Your name.*

Psalm 79:9

There are times in our lives when we feel desperate for God's help. Whether it's facing the news of a cancer diagnosis or dealing with a rebellious child, most of us struggle at some point to stay out of the pit of despair.

The psalmist encourages us that God has a vested interest in what happens to us and is concerned about how we handle situations. Because God's name is full of magnificence and splendor, He wants to preserve it!

Praying in God's name does not assure us that we'll avoid all difficulty. But asking Him to give us His comfort, encouragement, forgiveness, or support for the sake of His own dignity and integrity is a powerful way to pray!

Father,
We're grateful that You help us for the honor of Your name.
Amen.

July 30

"I Will Be with You"

But Moses protested to God, "Who am I to appear before Pharaoh? Who am I to lead the people of Israel out of Egypt?" God answered, "I will be with you."
Exodus 3:11-12

The man God chose to lead His people out of Egypt suffered from a major inferiority complex. When Moses looked around, he saw the terrible oppression of his people. When he looked within, he saw his weakness and inadequacy.

Because Moses' vision was limited to only what he could see horizontally, he asked God, "Who am I ...? Who am I ..." It's interesting that God didn't say, to Moses, "You can do it – you just need to believe in yourself." Instead, God asked Moses to expand his vision vertically by looking up to Him, and He promised He would be with Moses.

In order for us to move beyond the weakness and inadequacy within us and around us, we need to look up. God will be with us, too.

God,
Thank You for the assurance of Your presence. Amen.

August

A City Light

*"You are the light of the world – like a city on a hilltop
that cannot be hidden. No one lights a lamp and then
puts it under a basket. Instead, a lamp is placed on a stand,
where it gives light to everyone in the house. In the same
way, let your good deeds shine out for all to see,
so that everyone will praise your heavenly Father."*

Matthew 5:14-16

Standing a few blocks north of Oxford and Regents in central London is All Souls Church. For twenty-five years, John Stott was the rector of the church.

The unique building, designed by the famous architect John Nash, is a symbol of the bright spiritual life of the people of the church. With more than seventy nationalities participating in the congregation, the church's light spreads out into many corners of London's culture and beyond.

When we live in relationship with our heavenly Father, He shares His light with us – light that shines to those around us. Do we have a history of shining for Him?

Lord,
May I faithfully hold my light high, reflecting the light of Your glory. Amen.

August 1

Allegiance to God

"When you help the Hebrew women give birth, kill all the boys as soon as they are born." But because the midwives feared God, they refused to obey the kings. And because the midwives feared God, He gave them families of their own.

Exodus 1:16-17, 21

Two Hebrew midwives in the Old Testament book of Exodus illustrate that allegiance to God supersedes allegiance to people. When the king of Egypt wanted to wipe out some of the Hebrew population, he ordered two supervising midwives, Shiphrah and Puah, to kill all the baby boys.

These two women risked their lives and disobeyed Pharaoh's command out of respect for God. But God blessed their devotion to Him by giving them families of their own.

We may encounter situations where obeying God means not following another human authority. If we do, we can appeal to God for courage as we obey Him rather than human authority.

Father,
You are the ultimate authority, and for that we are grateful.
Please give us wisdom when authority issues are unclear to us.
Amen.

August 2

A Runaway Returns

I appeal to you to show kindness to my child, Onesimus.
Onesimus hasn't been of much use to you in the past,
but now he is very useful to both of us. I am sending him
back to you, and with him comes my own heart.
Philemon 10-12

Onesimus was a slave belonging to Philemon, but he ran away to escape his duties. When Onesimus the runaway encountered Paul, he also encountered Christ. Paul became his "father" in the faith.

Onesimus's conversion demonstrated two dimensions of spiritual transformation. First, he submitted himself to the obligation of his life and returned to his master. Second, he became "useful" to Philemon. Instead of avoiding his duties, he embraced them. His slavery became freedom – freedom to do what is right.

This is true for all of us who were once slaves to sin. We now have freedom – freedom that enables us to be useful servants of the gracious Father who has adopted us into His very own family.

Lord,
Thank You that while once I was a slave to sin, You have freed me to serve You. Amen.

August 3

Perfect Parent

God says, "At the time I have planned,
I will bring justice."
Psalm 75:2

Picture a little fella who's traveling on an airplane flight with his mother. During take-off and landing, he needs to be restrained by a seat belt attached to his mother's seat belt.

The wee lad kicks and screams because he's got places he'd like to go and people he'd like to see. Things just don't seem fair!

Sometimes, we struggle with the same feelings, *God, the situation I'm in doesn't seem fair!* Our heavenly Father assures us, though, that all issues of timing and justice are under His control. He is a perfect parent, and we can trust in His loving plan for our greater good.

Father,
May we rest in the assurance that Your plan is for our good.
Amen.

Flee ... to God

Potiphar's wife soon began to look at him lustfully. "Come and sleep with me," she demanded. But Joseph refused. She kept putting pressure on Joseph ... but he refused ... and he kept out of her way ... One day ... She came and grabbed him by his cloak, demanding, "Come on, sleep with me!" Joseph tore himself away ...

Genesis 39:7-12

Most of us know of friends or relatives who have been wounded by sexual sin. And none of us are strangers to temptations of sexual immorality, whether in thought or deed.

I'm grateful for examples of people throughout the Bible who were faced with various temptations and handled them well.

Notice the progressive nature of Joseph's decisions. He refused. He refused again and again. He kept out of Potiphar's wife's way. He fled. What a great pattern for each of us when we face temptations of any kind. Refuse. Refuse again. Keep out of the way. If necessary, flee!

Father,
We are grateful that You understand our temptations and have unlimited power to help us. Amen.

August 5

In the Desert

O God, You are my God; I earnestly search for You.
My soul thirsts for You; my whole body longs for You in
this parched and weary land where there is no water.

Psalm 63:1

The Sahara Desert is a daunting piece of land, stretching about 3,000 miles across the northern part of Africa. Measuring 3.5 million square miles, the Sahara is the largest desert in the world. It's probably also the hottest, since the Libyan section of the desert recorded a high of 136°F back in 1922.

Trying to picture the Sahara helps us identify with the words of the psalmist, "... in this parched and weary land where there is no water." The words have the ring of a desperate and dehydrated person.

Some of us may have been physically dehydrated before; but we can also become spiritually dehydrated, finding ourselves in parched and weary places. Like the psalmist, we can run to God, saying, "You are my God. My soul thirsts for You."

Father,
During dry times, may You quench our thirst. Amen.

August 6

The Only God

*If anyone comes to your meeting and does not teach
the truth about Christ, don't invite that person into your
home or give any kind of encouragement. Anyone who
encourages such people becomes a partner in their evil work.*
2 John 10-11

From time to time people come to our door offering religious literature that looks as though it comes from the Bible. Upon careful examination of the literature, we sometimes find it teaching that Jesus is merely a fine teacher or prophet.

John reminds his readers that a proper understanding of Jesus Christ is central to true faith in God. Jesus is the only Way to eternal life. From the earliest days of the Christian church, men and women have recognized the need to hold on to the truth about Christ. It's just as important for us to hold on to it today.

Lord,
Give me wisdom and perseverance to embrace the supremacy of Jesus Christ. Confirm in my heart that He is above everything in the universe, and help me to bow in humble worship at His feet. Amen.

August 7

Stones of Remembrance

*We will use these stones to build a memorial. In the
future your children will ask you, 'What do these stones
mean?' Then you can tell them, "They remind us that
the Jordan River stopped flowing when the Ark of the
L*ORD*'s covenant went across. These stones will stand
as a memorial among the people of Israel forever."*

Joshua 4:6-7

Just before Joshua led the people of Israel into the
Promised Land, he followed the Lord's instructions
to build a memorial in the middle of the Jordan
River. Here, the Israelites had miraculously crossed
the river when God stopped the flow of the water
and made the ground dry. The stones were to be a
reminder to the people and their children that God
is all-powerful, and that He alone should be feared.

What are the "stones of remembrance" in your
life? What are some of the ways in which God
has faithfully led you? Remembering these times
can be a great encouragement to us and others as
we share the good things God has done in our lives.

August 8

Lord,
Give me eyes to see Your faithfulness and share it with those
around me. Amen.

Ask for Help

Those who look to Him for help will be radiant with joy;
no shadow of shame will darken their faces.

Psalm 34:5

In order to unlock the door to your home or apartment, you need to use the proper key. If you struggle to find the right key, you may end up standing outside for a while.

Our search for joy seems to require a key as well, and when we struggle to find it, we sometimes feel as though we're "waiting outside." If you're straining to find joy today, set aside a quiet moment in a private setting where you can express your feelings, needs, and concerns to God.

God is willing to listen and understand. He's also willing to share His radiance and joy with us. Ask Him – He's ready to help.

Father,
We want to be joyful. We're grateful that You are willing to help us. Amen.

August 9

Eyes That See

*"Your eye is a lamp that provides light for your body.
When your eye is good, your whole body is filled with light.
But when it is bad, your body is filled with darkness."*

Luke 11:34

Recently, two physicians from the Wheaton Eye Clinic traveled to Sudan with a case that contained eleven eyeballs. The physicians were on a mission to replace the corneas of eleven waiting patients who were eager to receive new sight.

As a result of surgery, each of these people acquired vision to see things they had never been able to see before. When Jesus spoke to New Testament crowds, He encouraged them to gaze on God – the One who is able to bring us spiritual vision.

Focusing on God causes us to see right from wrong and helps us understand things we never understood before. As we fix our eyes on God, our lives are filled with light.

Lord,
You are the light of the world. Thank You that You open our eyes to Your truth. Amen.

August 10

Growing Wise

Anyone who rebukes a mocker will get an insult in return.
Anyone who corrects the wicked will get hurt.
So don't bother correcting mockers; they will only
hate you. But correct the wise, and they will love you.
Instruct the wise, and they will be even wiser.

Proverbs 9:7-9

How we react to a person who corrects or rebukes us indicates what kind of people we are. Do we listen carefully with willingness to be informed or taught, or do we outwardly (or inwardly) mock a person who corrects us?

Not all correction comes to us with kindness and respect. Sometimes people who "offer" us such gifts act unwisely themselves. Hopefully, that won't prevent us from looking for the grain of truth in their comments.

If we want to become wise, we must be willing to learn from correction. In so doing, we'll continue to grow wiser.

Father,
It's so easy to become defensive when someone corrects us.
Please help us to listen carefully instead. Amen.

August 11

Beautiful Bride

And I saw the holy city, the new Jerusalem,
coming down from God out of heaven like
a bride beautifully dressed for her husband.
Revelation 21:2

I will never forget the moment. Seated in a pew next to my husband, just minutes before our son's wedding, I heard the processional music begin. Everyone in the church stood and turned to gaze at Brit, Nate's beautiful bride. My breath caught in my chest, and a lump formed in my throat.

I hadn't anticipated how overcome I would feel. If any of us can feel that much emotion and excitement at a wedding ceremony here on earth, I can only imagine what it will be like when Christ, the Bridegroom of all bridegrooms, comes to claim His church, the Bride of all brides.

The awe we feel about Christ's redemptive love for us is a wonder that we will celebrate forever. It is above and beyond anything we can ever imagine!

Father,
We are grateful that in Your plans made long ago, You designed for the church to be Your bride. Amen.

God Supplies

And this same God who takes care of me [Paul]
will supply all your needs from His glorious riches,
which have been given to us in Christ Jesus.
Philippians 4:19

Before the beginning of a new school year, moms often take their children shopping for school supplies. Students need to be properly equipped before they can write a report, paint a picture, or figure out the hypotenuse of a triangle.

As adults, we sometimes wish that the provision of our needs was as simple. We're aware of our shortage of patience, our longing to be loved, or our feelings of inadequacy. Where do we go to get our needs met?

The apostle Paul lived through shipwreck, prison, hunger, and robbery. The Bible records that Paul experienced God's provisions in the midst of such challenges. God, who took care of Paul, will supply our needs too.

God,
We are needy people. We are grateful that You will supply our needs from Your abundant riches. Amen.

August 13

But God ...

*These patriarchs were jealous of their brother Joseph,
and they sold him to be a slave in Egypt. But God
was with him and rescued him from all his troubles.
And God gave him favor before Pharaoh.
God also gave Joseph unusual wisdom, so that
Pharaoh appointed him governor over all of Egypt.*

Acts 7:9-10

After Joseph's jealous brothers betrayed him by selling him to traders from another country, it seemed that he would never be heard from again. "But God ..." Those two little words are huge. But God what? God was with Joseph.

He showed him favor – He encouraged Joseph in the midst of his trouble. God gave him wisdom – He helped Joseph to interpret one of Pharaoh's dreams. God rescued Joseph – not immediately, but God protected him until He delivered him.

If you are discouraged about seemingly irreversible damages in your life or the life of someone you love, be encouraged. God is with us, He shows us favor, gives us wisdom, and rescues us.

God,
You were faithful to Joseph. We are encouraged to trust You, too. Amen.

August 14

Strength to Run

Even youths will become weak and tired, and
young men will fall in exhaustion. But those who trust
in the LORD will find new strength. They will run and not
grow weary. They will walk and not faint.

Isaiah 40:30-31

When our nephew Jeff first arrived at Wheaton College, he came a few weeks early for football practice. Training for the season was rigorous, and the incoming freshmen had to prove their endurance through a time trial on the running track

While Jeff easily completed the required circuits, some of his buddies struggled. I will never forget the sight of Jeff returning to the track, taking the arms of a friend who was on the verge of collapse, and virtually dragging him across the finish line.

There are times in life when even the strongest of us feel completely overwhelmed by our circumstances. That is time to trust in the Lord. He won't just drag us along, but promises to give us new strength, so that we can run without weariness!

Lord,
Thank You that You understand our weariness and weakness.
Please give us Your promised strength. Amen.

August 15

Tender Mercies

*LORD, don't hold back Your tender mercies from me.
Let Your unfailing love and faithfulness always
protect me. For troubles surround me – too many to count!
My sins pile up so high I can't see my way out. They
outnumber the hairs on my head. I have lost all courage.*

Psalm 40:11-12

The trouble that the psalmist's sins caused for him is not unfamiliar to us. Sometimes our sins pile up and tempt us to lose courage.

When sin threatened to overwhelm the psalmist, he cried out to God with a desperate prayer for deliverance. Acknowledging his spiritual need to God, he realized that only as he drew on God's unfailing love and faithfulness could he deal with the evil and sin that was around him and within him.

The psalmist's prayer in Psalm 40:17 is a fitting prayer for us, "As for me, since I am poor and needy, let the Lord keep me in His thoughts. You are my helper and my Savior. O my God, do not delay."

Lord,
We are in need of Your tender mercies. Please protect us with Your unfailing love. Amen.

August 16

His Heart Turned to God

*Never before had there been a king like Josiah,
who turned to the Lord with all his heart and soul
and strength, obeying all the laws of Moses.
And there has never been a king like him since.*
2 Kings 23:25

Josiah was one of Judah's most remarkable kings. Crowned at the age of eight, he reigned over the country for about thirty-one years. We are told that at the age of sixteen, he began to seek the God of his ancestor David.

As he matured, Josiah began a series of radical spiritual reforms. The turning point in his life seemed to be the discovery of the book of God's Law. Upon hearing all the ways in which his people had failed to obey God, Josiah was moved to despair.

He repented and turned wholeheartedly to God. We can do the same! God's Word is powerful. When we read His Word, repent, and turn to Him, He is faithful to guide us.

Lord,
Help me, like Josiah, to pay attention to Your Word. May I be ready to turn away from sin and turn toward You. Amen.

August 17

Facing Temptation

*During that time the devil came and said to Him,
"If You are the Son of God, tell these stones to become
loaves of bread." But Jesus told him, "No! The Scriptures
say, 'People do not live by bread alone, but by
every word that comes from the mouth of God.'"*

Matthew 4:3-4

Whenever we face temptation, it's encouraging to remember that Jesus faced temptation, too. While He lived on earth, He experienced the tugs of desire, power, and pride that are common to us all.

Although Jesus never sinned, He knows what it feels like to be tempted. He also demonstrated how to resist it – with the Word of God. If Jesus, the Son of God, needed God's Word to withstand temptation, how much more do you and I need it?

Jesus was saturated with God's Word. He was submissive to it as well. What a great pattern He left for the rest of us!

Father,
May we spend enough time reading the Bible so that when we feel the tug of temptation, we will remember Your words.
Amen.

August 18

Tell about God

*Moses told his father-in-law everything the LORD had done
to Pharaoh and Egypt on behalf of Israel. He also told about
all the hardships they had experienced along the way and
how the LORD had rescued His people from all their troubles.*

Exodus 18:8

As Moses told his father-in-law, Jethro, how God
had rescued the Israelites out of Egypt, he didn't
leave out the hardships. I like that because we have
hardships, too.

I would like to have listened to Moses' stories.
He probably related how terrified the people felt
when it appeared that the Egyptians had trapped
them. He probably described what the Red Sea
looked like when God parted the waters, giving
account of how Pharaoh and the Egyptians were
swallowed up.

What a great pattern Moses left us for telling
others what God has done in our lives. *Tell them
what He did. Don't leave out the hardships. Explain how
God rescued you from your troubles.*

Father,
May we be faithful to tell others about the ways You have
helped us. Amen.

August 19

Start Small

Get rid of all bitterness, rage, anger, harsh words,
and slander, as well as all types of evil behavior.
Instead, be kind to each other, tenderhearted, forgiving
one another, just as God through Christ has forgiven you.
Ephesians 4:31-32

What do getting rid of things and forgiving one another have in common? They're easier to do when the issues are small. Getting rid of weeds in a pot of geraniums takes seconds, but digging up a juniper tree takes hours.

Identifying and making an apology for one scathing remark is more manageable than sorting through and dealing with a lifetime of abusive talk. Forgiving a friend who forgot a lunch date doesn't require as much time or effort as forgiving a family member who betrayed us. Either way, we deal with one thing at a time.

If we deal with things while they are small, the benefits we reap will be huge. Through it all, we rely on the One who helps and forgives us.

Father,
Help us to deal with problems while they're still small. May we offer forgiveness to others as You have offered it to us. Amen.

Mighty Savior

*"For the LORD your God is living among you. He is
a mighty savior. He will take delight in you with
gladness. With His love, He will calm all your fears.
He will rejoice over you with joyful songs."*
Zephaniah 3:17

The Bible Club camp my husband attended as a
boy left a huge impression on his life. The camp's
leadership wanted kids to be transformed through
God's Word, so day by day they held morning and
evening chapel.

Jim still recalls the words of Zephaniah 3:17
emblazoned on a plaque that hung at the front of
the chapel. He read those verses over and over, not
realizing then how the truth of it would seep into
his soul.

Forty years later, he looks back and sees how God
has been a mighty Savior in his life. He has been
calmed by the quiet assurance of the Spirit, and has
experienced the pleasure of God's gladness!

Lord,
Thank You for the many ways You speak to us, Your children.
Let us never forget that You are a mighty Savior, and that You
take delight in us! Amen.

August 21

Facing Our Giants

*"But my servant Caleb has a different attitude
than the others have. He has remained loyal to Me,
so I will bring him into the land he explored.
His descendants will possess their full share of that land."*

Numbers 14:24

After fleeing from the slavery of Egypt, the Israelites came to the outskirts of Canaan, the land God had promised them. Wanting to know what they were up against, Moses sent twelve scouts into Canaan.

Ten scouts reported that they were intimidated by giants in the land. Those ten men saw themselves as grasshoppers. Yet two scouts returned believing that God would deliver Canaan into their hands. Caleb was one of them.

The ten who didn't believe God forfeited their opportunity to enter Canaan, but Caleb – forty years later – entered Canaan as a reward for his faith. We face giants in our lives too. Fear says "I'm little and the giants are big." Faith says "I'm little, but God is big."

Father,
As we look to You, please strengthen us to walk in faith, not fear. Amen.

August 22

Freed from Fears

I prayed to the LORD, and He answered me.
He freed me from all my fears.
Psalm 34:4

In our relationships with family and friends, perhaps nothing warms us more than knowing that someone cares about our feelings and our fears. Whether we're facing fears about work, health, or relationships, we feel affirmed and blessed when someone listens and seems to understand.

God stands way above any human being in His capacity to help. Not only does He understand what we fear – He also understands why we fear it. Not only does He understand how we need to be freed from those fears – He is the One who provides our freedom.

Whatever the degree of our fears – whether they are as mild as uneasiness or as intense as terror – He is the One who can still our fears, disentangle us from them, and set us free.

Lord,
Our fears sometimes threaten to paralyze us. We're grateful that we can come to You for help. Amen.

August 23

Awesome

*Come, everyone! Clap your hands! Shout to God
with joyful praise! For the LORD Most High is awesome.
He is the great King of all the earth.*

Psalm 47:1-2

It's curious that trendy words in our culture are often words that are found in the Bible. Take the word *awesome*, for example. Some years ago, it was popular (for some, it still is) to use the word awesome to describe a beautiful sunset or, when asked, "How are you?" to respond with "Awesome!"

Although I don't hear the word used as much in conversations these days, the Bible uses it frequently to describe God. There is nothing common, average, or ordinary about God. He is awesome. He is the Lord Most High.

For any fear or challenge you are facing today, remember that God is not weak, distant, or out of reach. He is the awesome King of all the earth.

Father,
We praise You because You – the Lord Most High – are awesome! Amen.

August 24

A Taste of Kindness

*Cry out for this nourishment, now that you
have had a taste of the Lord's kindness.*
I Peter 2:2-3

Spaghetti from Italy. Szechuan Chicken from China.
Chicken Tandori from India. A delightful gift from
our Creator, taste stimulates our appetites.

Sweet foods like grapes and strawberries taste
good because our bodies require sugars and carbohydrates. One bite of Mom's apple pie leaves us
longing for more! How gracious, then, that God
is not a stone idol to be looked at or a statue to be
bowed down to.

He is a living Spirit who can be tasted, appreciated, and relished, bringing us gladness, joy, and
satisfaction. Experience the nourishment of His
care. As we spend time in God's Word, we will
receive a taste of His kindness.

Lord,
The more time we spend in Your Word, the more we want to
spend time with You. Amen.

August 25

Light for the Path

*Your word is a lamp to guide my feet
and a light for my path.*
Psalm 119:105

If you've ever gone on a camping trip, you've probably packed a lantern or a flashlight. Whether you wanted to look for owls at midnight or thought you might need to get up with a small child before dawn, you realized you'd need a lantern.

Lanterns shine enough light to see a few steps ahead, helping us to avoid tripping over roots or falling into holes. God's Word does the same thing. Without it, we'd feel as though we were stumbling through a forest of dangers and pitfalls.

Unlike a floodlight that illuminates a whole landscape, a lantern provides just enough light for the next few steps. That's why we need God's Word constantly.

Father,
What would we do without Your Word? Thanks for equipping us for life's adventures. Amen.

August 26

Fulfilled Purposes

*Have mercy on me, O God, have mercy! I look to You for
protection. I will hide beneath the shadow of Your wings
until the danger passes by. I cry out to God Most High,
to God who will fulfill His purpose for me.*
Psalm 57:1-2

The psalmist realized that there was much to be
gained from spending time with God. Protection,
for one thing. That includes care, assurance, certainty, defense, refuge, safety, security, stability, and
strength. Who among us wouldn't like to experience more of these on a daily basis?

Another benefit the psalmist found in his relationship with God was purpose. The more time we
spend with God through His Word, the more we
realize that God has aims, intentions, designs, and
objectives for our lives.

As we look to Him and follow Him in faith, He
will accomplish and complete His purposes for us.
Through faith in Him, our lives will hit the target of
His purposes.

Father,
When things around us fall apart, we cling to the assurance
that You will fulfill Your purposes for us. Amen.

August 27

Proof of Repentance

"Prove by the way you live that you have repented of your sins and turned to God."

Luke 3:8

When we think of popular buzzwords in the world today like global, green peace, or recycle, it's unlikely that the word repentance would make the list. But that was the buzzword that came from the lips of John the Baptist as he prepared the way for Jesus.

It is a strong word, because it demands change. The crowds of John's day seemed more interested in performing certain rituals than in changing unhealthy behaviors. How can we avoid making the same mistake?

Repentance – real repentance – includes recognizing our wrong, desiring forgiveness, desiring God, and changing direction. If selfish behaviors in our lives aren't changing, then true repentance isn't happening. Repentance is proven by the way we live.

Father,
We want our lives to bear the fruit of repentance. Amen.

August 28

Joshua Fit the Battle ...

But the LORD said to Joshua, "I have given you Jericho,
its king, and all its strong warriors."
Joshua 6:2

From east to west, the story of the "battle of Jericho" is well known to young and old alike. The children sing, "Joshua fit the battle of Jericho," while skeptics argue over the archeological evidence.

Though ample evidence does exist to validate the event, thinking of Jericho in those terms may overshadow the real point of the story. God was the one who fought for Joshua and the people of Israel.

It was not by their power or numbers that they won the battle. It was God's strength that caused the walls to fall and won the day. And so it is in our lives as we face difficult or insurmountable problems. It is the power and grace of God that enables us to overcome.

Lord,
Deliver us from the notion that we can overcome life's obstacles in our own power. Help us be quick to look to You for help and strength. Amen.

August 29

Anchored

*We who have fled to Him for refuge can have great
confidence as we hold to the hope that lies before us.
This hope is a strong and trustworthy anchor for our souls.*
Hebrews 6:18-19

In order for the captain of a large ship to anchor his
vessel securely, he needs several things: a reliable
anchor, a method of attaching a cable from the
anchor of the ship, accurate charts, and a way to
measure the water's depth.

Living confidently in this world requires similar
things. The Bible explains how to find a strong and
trustworthy anchor for our souls. Flee to God. How
do we attach to Him? Through faith!

And what about charts – how do we navigate?
That's where His Word comes in. In God's Word,
we learn which direction to follow as well as which
places and depths to avoid. He will help us know
how to move ahead as we rely on Him.

Father,
In an unpredictable world, we're thankful that You are a firm
anchor. Amen.

August 30

Too Many Warriors?

*The LORD said to Gideon, "You have too many warriors
with you. If I let all of you fight the Midianites,
the Israelites will boast to Me that they saved
themselves by their own strength."*

Judges 7:2

Conventional military wisdom teaches the use of
superior force against one's enemies. In the story
of Gideon's battle against the armies of Midian,
however, God had a very different plan. The Bible
explains exactly why – pride!

If the people of Israel had gone up against the
other army in their strength, God knew they would
have been tempted to take credit for the victory. So
He told Gideon to reduce his army from over 32,000
to 300, in order to fight an army of 135,000.

Too often, we try to win battles in our own
strength, failing to turn to God for His help.
Gideon's great victory stands as a reminder that
when God gives us a task, He will provide for us
in every way.

Lord,
Thank You for Your strength and victory day by day. Amen.

August 31

September

"Geborgenheit"

*But as for me I will sing about Your power. Each morning I
will sing with joy about Your unfailing love. For You have
been my refuge, a place of safety when I am in distress.*
Psalm 59:16

Think of a place where you feel safe and secure.
Some of you might reflect on a childhood home.
Perhaps others conjure up the image of a lakefront
pier where they like to sit and read.

The German language has a word for such a
place – *geborgenheit*. It's a place of safety or security.
In this world of stress, difficulty, and sometimes
even despair, God Himself has offered to be our *geborgenheit* – our place of safety and security.

Find a quiet spot today where you can talk to
God about your particular challenges. Tell Him ex-
actly how you are feeling, because He cares. Thank
Him that He has promised to be your *geborgenheit*.

Father,
Thank You that even in the midst of distress, we can find our
safety in You. Amen.

September 1

Belonging

For you are all children of God through faith in
Christ Jesus. And now that you belong to Christ,
you are the true children of Abraham. You are his heirs,
and God's promise to Abraham belongs to you.

Galatians 3:26, 29

When I discovered that I had made the final tryouts for the Rhythmettes, I was ecstatic. The only thing better than making it into the group of high-school pom-pom girls, was the fact that I got to wear my Rhythmette sweater to school each Friday.

The sense of belonging that I felt was palpable. Although I shed my Rhythmette sweater many years ago, I haven't shed my need for belonging. Thankfully, that need is met daily through my relationship with Christ – a relationship I don't need to "try out" for.

When we place our faith in Christ, we become God's children. As His children, we are given His Spirit, bringing us a sense of belonging not just now, but forever.

Father,
We're thankful for the privilege of belonging to You. Amen.

September 2

What God Requires

"And now, Israel, what does the LORD your God
require of you? He requires only that you fear the LORD
your God, and live in a way that pleases Him,
and love Him and serve Him with all your heart and soul.
And you must always obey the LORD's commands."

Deuteronomy 10:12

Life is full of requirements. To set up a savings account at the bank, we're required to keep a certain amount of money in the account at all times.

When we show up at the airport for an international flight, we're required to show a picture ID and passport. Schools require birth certificates before children can be enrolled for classes.

God has requirements too. What He asks from us is our reverence, along with a desire to please Him, love Him, serve Him, and obey Him.

God's requirements are refreshing, because they have nothing to do with policies. They focus on our hearts and are there for our own good.

Father,
May we love You and serve You with grateful hearts. Amen.

September 3

Taste Test

Taste and see that the LORD is good.
Oh, the joys of those who take refuge in Him!
Psalm 34:8

When I serve my favorite chicken and stuffing casserole to dinner guests, they often say "This is delicious!" Once they've tasted it, it's not unusual for them to ask for a second helping.

Isn't it curious that the Bible says we can taste God? Instead of picking up a fork, we pick up His Word and discover that He is awesome. Once we see how wonderful He is and begin to receive nourishment from Him, our appetite increases and we want to spend more time tasting Him through reading His Word and talking to Him in prayer.

Just as a delicious meal brings joy to the one who consumes it, a taste of God brings joy to our hearts.

Father,
Thanks for tastes of Your goodness each day. Amen.

Bringing People to Jesus

Jesus returned to the Sea of Galilee and climbed a hill and sat down. A vast crowd brought to Him people who were lame, blind, crippled, those who couldn't speak, and many others. They laid them before Jesus, and He healed them all.
Matthew 15:29-30

It's significant to note the kinds of people that the crowd brought to Jesus. It wasn't the wealthy, the powerful, or the healthy. The crowd brought needy people to Jesus – people who were unable to walk, unable to speak, or unable to see.

As we follow Christ, we have opportunities to bring people to Him, too. Each of us knows friends or family members who are suffering, whether physically, spiritually, or emotionally.

We can pray for or with them, and we can tell them what Christ has done for us. Who are we seeking to bring to Christ?

Father,
Thank You for the care You have shown to us in our times of need. We want others to experience that care, too. Amen.

September 5

A Private Garden

You are my private garden, my treasure, my bride,
a secluded spring, a hidden fountain.
Song of Songs 4:12

Before a recent trip to London, I told my friend Julie that my husband and I would be staying close to Kensington Park. "If you have time," Julie said, "look for the private garden in Kensington Park."

Sure enough, my husband and I found the private garden on a Sunday afternoon stroll through the park. Bright flowers, bubbling fountains, and immaculate hedges surrounded the private, well-tended area.

A private garden is one image the Song of Songs uses to picture the intimate relationship between husband and wife. Private gardens are secluded, hidden, and special. So is the intimate relationship between husband and wife. For those of us who are married, it's good to ponder how we are tending and protecting our private gardens.

Father,
We're grateful for images in Your Word that help us understand how exclusive the marriage relationship is. Help us to tend it well. Amen.

September 6

God's Grants

*You will show me the way of life, granting me the joy
of Your presence and the pleasures of living with You forever.*
Psalm 16:11

Each year in the United States, approximately 350 billion dollars in grants are distributed to various U. S. citizens. Donated by the government, private foundations, or corporations, grants provide people with education, business, and housing opportunities that might otherwise have been difficult to realize.

In order to apply for a grant, a person needs to be a U. S. citizen and a taxpayer. He or she also needs to fill out extensive applications. It's refreshing to think that God's grants require no application process and that people from any country can approach Him.

When we enter into a relationship with God through faith in Christ, He grants us the joy of His presence and the pleasure of living with Him forever – all of this while He's showing us the way of life!

Father,
You are so generous. We're grateful that Your grants are available to everyone. Amen.

September 7

He Understands

Then Jesus shouted, "Father, I entrust My spirit into Your hands!" And with those words He breathed His last.
Luke 23:46
So if you are suffering in a manner that pleases God, keep on doing what is right, and trust your lives to the God who created you, for He will never fail you.
I Peter 4:19

When we experience the pain or grief of something that doesn't feel "fair", where do we turn? No one understands pain, grief, or unfair treatment more than Jesus.

In His agonizing moments on the cross, while dying for my sins and yours, Jesus entrusted Himself to God. It's comforting to us that He knows how suffering feels.

Beyond that, Jesus also left us instructions on how to deal with it. Through Peter, He encouraged us to keep doing what is right and trust ourselves to the God who created us. The best part of His encouragement is His promise. He will never fail us.

Father,
Thank You that You understand our pain. We entrust ourselves to You. Amen.

September 8

God Still Guides

*"Who is like You among the gods, O Lord – glorious
in holiness, awesome in splendor, performing
great wonders? You raised Your right hand, and the earth
swallowed our enemies. With Your unfailing love
You lead the people You have redeemed. In Your might,
You guide them to Your sacred home."*

Exodus 15:11-13

Those of you who enjoy watching sports on television probably remember a stunning turnaround at the end of some particular game or event. Wherever you went the next day, it's likely that people were still talking about the amazing victory (or defeat).

Even though thousands of years have passed since God parted the waters of the Red Sea, the wonder and excitement of the account has not diminished. That's good, because we need reminders of God's greatness and glory – especially at times when we face disturbing events in our lives.

God still leads His people with unfailing love. He still redeems. He still guides His people with might. There is no one like God.

Father,
We want to be led by Your unfailing love, too. Amen.

September 9

Ways to Wisdom

"They hated knowledge and chose not to fear the LORD. *They rejected My advice and paid no attention when I corrected them. Fools are destroyed by their own complacency. But all who listen to Me will live in peace, untroubled by fear of harm."*

Proverbs 1:29-30, 32-33

Look in any bookstore, and you'll find books with titles like *Four Habits to Help You Succeed in Life.* The verses from Proverbs (above) could prompt such a book.

It might be titled *Three Steps to Wisdom and Three Steps to Foolishness.* The way to wisdom? Fear God, pay attention to correction, and listen to the voice of wisdom. The way to foolishness? Hate knowledge, reject advice and correction, and be complacent.

Foolish living brings destruction. Wise living leaves us untroubled by fear of harm. The choice is up to us.

Father,
Your Word is full of principles and truths that point us to wise living. Please help us to heed them. Amen.

September 10

New Life

Yes, Adam's one sin brings condemnation for everyone, but Christ's one act of righteousness brings a right relationship with God and new life for everyone. Because one person disobeyed God, many became sinners. But because one other person obeyed God, many will be made righteous.

Romans 5:18-19

It's curious that we don't talk much about sin, since all of us are born with a tendency to do it. Traced back to the first person who ever lived, Adam's disobedience to God then is the reason why each of us deals with sin now.

One of the reasons we don't talk much about sin is because sin brought with it death, and death is bad news. But Christ brought Good News. When He died for our sins and rose again, He made it possible for us to live righteously – forever – through faith in Him.

The choice is ours. We can stand in the shadow of Adam and his sin, or we can walk in the light of Christ and His righteousness. Who will we follow?

Father,
We're thankful that we can have new life through You. Amen.

September 11

Reading, Writing, and ... Obedience

He must always keep that copy with him ... and read it daily as long as he lives. That way he will learn to fear the LORD his God by obeying ... these instructions ... This regular reading will prevent him from becoming proud.

Deuteronomy 17:18-20

When I was a child in school, the three main principles of education were sometimes referred to as "reading, writing, and arithmetic". When Moses spoke to the children of Israel about educating their leaders, the three principles he addressed were reading, writing, and ... obedience.

The most important part of a leader's education was to be instruction from God's Word. Back in those days, a leader had to copy Scripture one word at a time – by himself! Then he was to read it every day and obey it.

This, Moses said, would prevent the leaders from becoming proud and from turning away from God. Spending time daily in God's Word does the same for us – and we don't need to copy it by hand.

Father,
Thank You that Your Word is readily available to us. May we read it and obey it. Amen.

September 12

Surrounded

Many sorrows come to the wicked, but unfailing love surrounds those who trust the LORD. So rejoice in the LORD and be glad, all you who obey Him! Shout for joy, all you whose hearts are pure!
Psalm 32:10-11

If you were to visit the Caribbean island of Aruba, located about 15 miles north of Venezuela, the locals would recommend that you try scuba diving. On the Arashi dive, for example, you would be surrounded by parrot fish and angel fish.

If you explored the Antilla Wreck – a 400 ft. long German freighter that sunk in 1945 – lobsters and yellow tails would swim around you. To be enveloped by these gorgeous creatures that God made would be a breathtaking experience.

God assures us that when we trust Him, we are surrounded by His unfailing love. We don't need a scuba dive to experience that. We can trust God and be hemmed in by His love absolutely anywhere in the world.

Father,
We're grateful that Your unfailing love surrounds us. Amen.

September 13

Showing Care

"I was hungry, and you fed Me. I was thirsty, and you gave Me a drink. I was a stranger, and you invited Me into your home. I was naked, and you gave Me clothing. I was sick, and you cared for Me. I was in prison, and you visited Me."
Matthew 25:35-36

Feeding a hungry child. Showing hospitality to a stranger. Offering clothes to a street person. Caring for a cancer patient. Visiting a prisoner. Each of these actions show care to a person.

Each of these actions, said Jesus, show that we care about God's Kingdom. They're the kinds of things that God's Spirit prompts us to do when we've repented of our sins and put our trust in Christ.

When we want to demonstrate our love for God, we do it by showing love to family, friends, and strangers. The real evidence of how much we love God is shown by how we treat the people around us.

Father,
We confess times when we have been hardened to the needs of those around us. Please help us to honor You by showing care to others. Amen.

September 14

With Us

*During the night God spoke to him [Jacob] in a vision.
"I am God, the God of your father," the voice said. "Do not
be afraid to go down to Egypt, for there I will make your
family into a great nation. I will go with you down to Egypt."*
Genesis 46:2-4

It's curious that Old Testament Jacob – who early on
was a "homebody" – ended up becoming a world
traveler. Not that he particularly wanted to. After
deceiving his brother Esau and stealing Esau's
birthright, Jacob fled to Haran, the first of many
journeys in his lifetime.

The last journey of his life took him to Egypt,
to be reunited with his son Joseph who he thought
was dead. "Do not be afraid to go," God said to
"homebody" Jacob, "I will be with you."

What new experience or challenge in your life
is moving you out of your comfort zone? Take
your fears to God and trust Him to help you walk
through them. He was with Jacob, and He will be
with you.

Father,
In our comings and goings, we're grateful that You are with
us. Amen.

September 15

God Cares about Feelings

The LORD is close to the brokenhearted;
He rescues those whose spirits are crushed.

Psalm 34:18

Never in the Bible have I read instructions to stop crying, ignore my feelings, or pretend that everything's fine when it isn't. Rather, I regularly come across characters like Joseph, Ruth, Hannah, and David who express feelings that I identify with.

When the psalmist declares that God is close to people who are brokenhearted, he's not referring to people who are mildly sad. Brokenhearted people often feel devastated and grief-stricken – perhaps even despairing. And those who are crushed? That describes how we feel if our spirits have been trampled, humiliated, or mortified. I'm incredibly grateful that God does not find our deep and raw feelings unsettling or distasteful, but that He understands and is ready to help us.

Lord,
Thank You that You don't move away from us when we feel crushed. We're grateful that it's safe to come to You because You care about us. Amen.

September 16

Adopted

God decided in advance to adopt us into His own family by bringing us to Himself through Jesus Christ. This is what He wanted to do, and it gave Him great pleasure.

Ephesians 1:5-6

The loving parents of our delightful daughter-in-law, Brit, adopted her as an infant from Colombia, South America. Brit's parents say, with a twinkle in their eyes, "She was expensive to get, expensive to raise, and expensive to give away!"

Adoption is an expensive, time-consuming, and challenging adventure. In the Bible, the concept of adoption has great significance, referring to one of the greatest blessings of our heavenly Father.

Spiritually speaking, God transfers us from the family of disobedience to God's family, but there's no money or effort involved.

Through Christ's redeeming love, we've been brought into God's family to become His very own children.

Loving Father,
Some parents have traveled to other countries to adopt children. You went to the cross to adopt us. We praise You for such incredible love. Amen.

September 17

A Glorious Appearance

The priests could not enter the Temple of the LORD
because the glorious presence of the LORD filled it.
2 Chronicles 7:2

The magnificent temple that Solomon built was prominently located at the high point of Jerusalem. Worshipers traveled there to make their sacrifices and meet with God.

The most dramatic part of the temple's dedication was the moment fire flashed down from heaven, and the glorious appearance of the Lord filled the temple! Today, we no longer need a temple where we go to meet God – that need changed after the death and resurrection of Jesus.

Now, God's Spirit comes to live in us when we trust Christ, and we become the temple of God. The character and works of God can be seen in us! No wonder God asks us to take care of His temple.

Lord,
Help me today to take great care of Your temple, keeping it clean and beautiful. I want others to see Your glorious presence. For Jesus' sake. Amen.

September 18

Unwavering Faith

When you ask Him, be sure that your faith is in God alone. Do not waver, for a person with divided loyalty is as unsettled as a wave of the sea that is blown and tossed by the wind.

James 1:6

One thing my family enjoys about ocean vacations is "catching" waves and riding them to the shore. Windy days make it particularly fun. The waves are unpredictable because the wind is constantly changing.

While unpredictable waves might provide fun at the ocean, unpredictable faith causes a lot of anxiety. Living with a divided heart makes us as agitated, unbalanced, and variable as a wave of the sea.

If we want to avoid an indecisive life, it's good to ask God for His wisdom and place our faith in Him alone.

Father,
An unsettled life is not fun. We want to live with unwavering faith in You. Amen.

September 19

See for Yourself

*"What sorrow awaits you who say to wooden idols,
'Wake up and save us!' Can an idol tell you what to do?
They may be overlaid with gold and silver, but they are
lifeless inside. But the Lord is in His holy Temple.
Let all the earth be silent before Him."*

Habakkuk 2:19-20

It's ironic that we spend so much time pursuing things that can't help us or respond to us. Idols – things other than God that receive worship – were blatant in Moses and Elijah's times.

Today, idols may not seem quite so obvious. They tend to look more like jobs, cars, houses, and sexual immorality. Idols have no breath, but God Almighty spoke the world into existence with His breath. Idols have no life, but Everlasting God gives eternal and abundant life. Idols have no ears to hear us when our hearts are breaking, but God listens and comforts us through His Word and His Spirit.

Unlike idols, God is real and powerful. As we read His Word, we see that for ourselves.

Almighty God,
May we quiet our hearts before You – the One who helps us.
Amen.

September 20

God Will Help

Then the Lord asked Moses, "Who makes a person's mouth?
Who decides whether people speak or do not speak,
hear or do not hear, see or do not see? Is it not I,
the Lord? Now go! I will be with you as you speak,
and I will instruct you in what to say."

Exodus 4:11-12

Moses' hesitation and insecurity were understandable. God wanted Moses to visit the king of Egypt, seek the release of the Hebrew people from captivity, and lead them out of Egypt.

Seeing how God dealt with Moses' fears and insecurities is helpful to us, because we have our own. God didn't reassure Moses that he was tremendously capable. What God did assure Moses of was that He would be with him.

God didn't focus on the what – the task. He focused on the Who – Him! He promised Moses that He would be with him and He would instruct him. God, who promised to be with Moses, promises to be with us, too.

God,
You are totally dependable. Please help us to rest in Your promises. Amen.

September 21

Opportunities for Growth

Dear brothers and sisters, when troubles come your way, consider it an opportunity for great joy. For you know that when your faith is tested, your endurance has a chance to grow. So let it grow, for when your endurance is fully developed, you will be perfect and complete, needing nothing.

James 1:2-4

"Think of it as an adventure." It is a phrase my husband and I sometimes repeat when things go wrong. Whether it's a flat tire, a plumbing problem, or a delayed flight, in our better moments we try to find some thread of humor in the problem.

We don't always react positively to challenges, though. Some events test our faith and endurance. It's realistic of James to remind us that it's not a matter of whether troubles might come our way. It's a matter of when.

Each trouble is an opportunity for growth in character. Thankfully, God is not aloof from us in our troubles. He is with us, and He will help us. In our testing, He will strengthen us to endure.

Father,
Sometimes, our endurance wanes. Please strengthen us and encourage us. Amen.

September 22

God's Love and Concern

*Then the people of Israel were convinced that the L*ORD *had sent Moses and Aaron. When they heard that the L*ORD *was concerned about them and had seen their misery, they bowed down and worshiped.*

Exodus 4:31

Before the great Exodus – when Moses led the Hebrew people out of Egyptian slavery – what did it take to convince the people of Israel that God was concerned about them? The same thing that it takes for us – a miracle!

Actually, God gave them several miracles. He turned Moses' staff into a snake, turned it back into a staff, made one of Moses' hands leprous, and instantly healed it. God gave His people a miracle to assure them that He cared about them.

He has done the same for us. He sent His sinless Son, Jesus, to live on earth, die horrifically for our sins, and rise to conquer sin and death. If that miracle doesn't convince us of God's great love and concern for us, I don't know what will.

Father,
Only You would go to such lengths to show us love. We thank You and praise You. Amen.

September 23

100% Reliable

The LORD merely spoke, and the heavens were created.
He breathed the word, and all the stars were born.
He assigned the sea its boundaries and
locked the oceans in vast reservoirs.
Psalm 33:6-7

Have you ever set a date to have breakfast with someone ... and forgotten to show up? It's a humbling experience. I'd rather be the one waiting than the one who forgets.

As much as I strive to be a dependable person, I realize that this side of heaven no one is 100% reliable – except God. God is faithful. God is steadfast. God is trustworthy.

Anyone who can speak the heavens into being, birth the stars with a breath, assign boundaries to the seas and lock oceans into vast reservoirs is Someone that I can depend on. It's awesome to realize that my Creator and Sustainer is totally reliable.

God,
We are awed to think that we can have a relationship with You – the Creator of the universe! Amen.

September 24

Defend the Faith

Dear friends, I had been eagerly planning to write to you about the salvation we all share. But now I find that I must write about something else, urging you to defend the faith that God has entrusted once for all time to His holy people.

Jude 3

DE-FENSE, DE-FENSE, CLAP-CLAP, clap-clap-clap. At basketball games, we often hear these words chanted by cheerleaders on the sidelines of the gym. In the second-to-last book of the Bible, though, the cheerleader was Jude, and his tone of rallying people to defense was surprisingly sober.

Bottom line, Jude reminded his readers – including us – that what we believe about God determines the way we live. And what we believe about God depends on what we know from His Word.

God's truth points us to Jesus while it defends us from false teachings that could creep in and derail us. Our defense is the Bible, which helps us not to drift away from Christ.

Father,
May we not drift from Your Word, because it points us to Christ. Amen.

Determined

The gracious hand of his God was on him.
This was because Ezra had determined to study
and obey the Law of the LORD and to teach
those decrees and regulations to the people of Israel.

Ezra 7:9-10

When we think of Bible characters who demonstrated their commitment to God, Abraham, John the Baptist, and Paul come to mind. We're not so quick, though, to recall Ezra.

A powerful and faithful prophet, Ezra taught God's people through his words and through his life. God used Ezra to lead a group of exiles from Babylon to Jerusalem. At the time, Ezra probably wasn't aware of the impact his ministry would continue to have on his nation.

The key to Ezra's effectiveness was his commitment to God's Word. He faithfully studied it, and he was determined to obey it. When we are committed to studying and obeying God's Word, there is no limit to how God will use us.

Father,
Thank You for Your gracious hand on our lives. May we faithfully study and obey Your Word. Amen.

September 26

Lessons from a Dove

As Jesus came up out of the water,
He saw the heavens splitting apart and the
Holy Spirit descending on Him like a dove.
Mark 1:10

Doves appear early in the Bible, gracing its pages with important tasks. In Genesis, Noah sent out a dove to see if there was any dry land. In Leviticus, the people of Israel brought doves as burnt offerings to the Lord.

Doves are gentle birds that coo, stroke one another, and mate for life. They are defenseless, and do not resist even an attack on their young.

As Jesus came up out of the water after John baptized Him, the Spirit of God descended on Him in the form of a dove.

Perhaps God would be pleased if our lives more closely resembled the dove's – touched by God's Spirit, ready to sacrifice, humble, gentle, and faithful to serve.

Lord,
You have created all things for Your pleasure and service. Help me to learn some lessons from Your creatures – the humble doves. Amen.

September 27

Glory Like the Sea

*As the waters fill the sea, the earth will be filled
with an awareness of the glory of the LORD.*
Habakkuk 2:14

When I fly from London to Chicago, a good portion of the eight-hour flight is spent over the Atlantic Ocean. It's a big pond.

The Old Testament prophet Habakkuk compares God's glory to water that fills the sea. The question that springs to my mind is, "How much water is in the sea?" A lot.

Approximately 326 million trillion gallons (that includes eighteen zeros) of water can be found on the earth, and 98% of the earth's water is found in the oceans!

If 98% of the earth's water is stored in the oceans, and God's glory is likened to the fullness of the oceans, how much time do I spend thinking about the glory of God?

Father,
Your glory is astounding. May Habakkuk's comparison inspire me to think more about Your glory. Amen.

September 28

God Knows Everything

You know what I am going to say even before I say it, LORD.
You go before me and follow me. You place Your hand
of blessing on my head. Such knowledge is too
wonderful for me, too great for me to understand.

Psalm 139:4-6

God knows what I'm going to say before I've even said it. That means He also knows the things I almost said. That's sobering.

Sometimes I shy away from letting people get close to me because I'm afraid that they might not like what they see. But God – who knows me better than I even know myself – accepts me and loves me completely. That's comforting.

To think that we can have a personal relationship with a God who knows everything and is everywhere at once is beyond comprehension. But we can. The more we get to know Him, the more we want to trust Him with our thoughts, our concerns, and our questions. After all, He already knows them.

Father,
You are too wonderful for us to understand, which is why we worship You. Amen.

September 29

Innovations

This same Good News that came to you is going out all over the world. It is bearing fruit everywhere by changing lives, just as it changed your lives from the day you first heard and understood the truth about God's wonderful grace.

Colossians 1:6

Once a month, I schedule a visit to Innovations – a local hair salon in Winfield, Illinois. Each time Robin trims and colors my hair, I look better than I did when I stepped in the door. That's because a change has taken place.

It's refreshing to enjoy a temporary change on the outside. It's even better to experience life-changing transformation that happens from the inside out. God's truth produces innovations that last.

As we spend time in His Word, He changes our attitudes, desires, thoughts, and behaviors. It doesn't happen all at once. Lasting change rarely does. But as we seek God's Word to guide us and the Holy Spirit to help us, we become less self-centered and more like Christ.

Father,
We're grateful that Your Word and Your Spirit help us to change and become more like You. Amen.

September 30

October

Anxious Thoughts

Search me, O God, and know my heart; test me and know my anxious thoughts. Point out anything in me that offends You, and lead me along the path of everlasting life.
Psalm 139:23-24

Do you ever feel anxious? Do you ever feel restless, nervous, or fearful? If you find yourself identifying with the psalmist's anxious thoughts, be encouraged by the pattern he left for dealing with them.

Ask God to search and know the most intimate and private part of you – your heart. Don't stop there. Courageously ask God to point out anything offensive in you – anything displeasing, insulting, or disturbing.

Our natural bent is to ignore or hide offensive things, but our willingness to have God call attention to our offenses is the first step towards health. Finally, admit that you need help and ask God to be your Shepherd. The path He will lead you on will never end, but the anxious thoughts will.

Father,
We bring our hearts to You, knowing that only You can deal properly with our anxiety. Please help us to shed our fears as we keep our eyes on You. Amen.

God's Way

"Refusing to accept God's way, they cling to their own way of getting right with God by trying to keep the law. For Christ has already accomplished the purpose for which the law was given. As a result, all who believe in Him are made right with God."

Romans 10:3-4

While I was a youngster attending school, my father gave me some wise advice. "Listen carefully," he said, "to your teacher's expectations. Concentrate on what's most important to your teacher."

If my teacher had wanted me to spend time listening to her but I chose to run errands for the principal instead, I would have been setting my own agenda – not co-operating with my teacher.

It's easy for us to miss God's intentions for our lives as well. No amount of good works or efforts on our part will make us right with God. When we see that it's not our efforts that earn us a relationship with God, we realize how gracious it is that He asks us to put our faith in His righteousness.

Father,
We're grateful that coming into a relationship with You doesn't depend on our efforts. Amen.

October 2

Fixed Thoughts

Fix your thoughts on what is true, and honorable and right, and pure, and lovely, and admirable. Think about things that are excellent and worthy of praise.

Philippians 4:8

Input determines output. It's true in finances, education, and computer programming. It's especially true with regard to our thoughts. The things we think about have direct bearing on our attitudes, words, and actions.

Thoughts are a little like the wind; we can't see the wind, but we can certainly see its effects. We can't measure a thought the way we can measure an earthquake, but thoughts can be powerful too – for good or for bad.

The Bible uses a powerful word to instruct us about our thoughts. We're to fix them – anchor, cement, fasten or secure them – to things that are honorable, right, pure, lovely, and admirable. That kind of thinking makes for healthy output.

Father,
It's so easy for our thoughts to flit all over the place. Please strengthen us as we purpose to fix our thoughts on good things. Amen.

October 3

The Great Awakening

"If My people who are called by My name will humble themselves and pray and seek My face and turn from their wicked ways, I will hear from heaven and will forgive their sins and restore their land."

2 Chronicles 7:14

In 1857, three men from New York City decided they were going to begin praying daily for revival. Soon, they were joined by dozens more. In a brief period of time, more than ten thousand people came to faith in Jesus Christ.

Over eight months, that number grew to fifty-thousand and eventually the revival spread to Ireland, Scotland, England, South Africa, and India. It became known as "The Great Awakening."

What is it that causes God to awaken people to their sin and turn to Him in repentance and faith? God's hand is moved by those who humbly pray, repent, and seek Him.

Lord,
May I be diligent in turning from anything that displeases You.
I come to You seeking Your power and provision. Amen.

October 4

Stick with the Herd

Stay alert! Watch out for your great enemy, the devil.
He prowls around like a roaring lion, looking for
someone to devour. Stand firm against him, and be strong
in your faith. Remember that your Christian brothers
and sisters all over the world are going through
the same kind of suffering you are.
2 Peter 5:8

Perhaps you have watched a television program documenting lions in their natural habitat. It's exciting – yet chilling – to observe a lion stalking its prey.

When a lion is on the prowl, what kind of animal does it look to devour? Most likely it's an animal that is alone, straggling behind the herd. In God's family, people who try to go it alone often make themselves vulnerable to the enemy of their souls.

God, in His wisdom, has designed for us to encourage, support, and protect one another. When we stay integrated in God's family, we find pleasure in the safety and beauty of the "herd."

Lord,
Give me the wisdom to value the family You have designed for my safety, well-being, and joy. Amen.

October 5

Uncountable Books

*Jesus also did many other things. If they were
all written down, I suppose the whole world
could not contain the books that would be written.*

John 21:25

The Bodleian Library at Oxford has been in use since
1602. With roots going back to the 14th century, it is
one of the largest libraries in Europe – a copyright
depository of the United Kingdom.

Today, the library group manages more than 8
million items on 117 miles of shelving. The vastness
of this particular collection stretches our imaginations. As the apostle John reflected on the works of
Jesus, he expressed similar amazement. His gospel
book contained only some of the stories of Jesus'
actions.

While we may have a hint at the vastness of
Christ's work, someday we will be utterly amazed
when we see Him face to face and learn of all He
has been doing.

Lord,
Thank You that Your great work includes knowing and caring
about me. Help me to live in this confidence. Amen.

October 6

God's Delight

He takes no pleasure in the strength of a horse or in human might. No, the Lord's delight is in those who fear Him, those who put their hope in His unfailing love.

Psalm 147:10-11

When God looks at us, what are some of the things that bring Him pleasure and delight? What does He enjoy seeing in us?

Even though we humans tend to pride ourselves on strength of intellect, power, money, or fitness, it's not our strengths that delight God. It's fear. "Fear?" you ask, yes, fear.

But not the kind of fear that sends us running. Rather, it's the kind of healthy reverence that sees God for who He is and responds to Him with reverent and affectionate obedience.

When we catch sight of God's unfailing love and compassion, we respond to Him with a hopeful fear that sends us into His arms. God delights in those who reverence Him.

Father,
Help us to focus more on showing You reverence than on working hard to be "strong". Amen.

October 7

Seed Multiplication

*"The seed that fell on good soil represents those
who truly hear and understand God's word
and produce a harvest of thirty, sixty, or even
a hundred times as much as had been planted!"*
Matthew 13:23

A visit to my brother-in-law's wheat farm in Kansas provided a refreshing contrast to my family's urban lifestyle. When harvest time came, we watched combines in the fields gather wheat that had grown from planted seeds.

In New Testament times, Jesus spoke to a crowd of people who were familiar with farming. But not all of them understood the spiritual principle Jesus taught about God's Word. He wanted them to know that when God's truth landed on someone's ears, it produced differing responses based on their readiness to accept truth.

How glad God is when we scatter the seed of His Word and the waiting soil of a person's heart yields an abundant life of godliness!

Lord,
May my heart be a place where Your Word takes root, grows strong, and produces a harvest of abundance. Amen.

October 8

God Directs

The LORD, the God of heaven, has ... appointed me to build Him a Temple at Jerusalem ... Any of you who are His people may go to Jerusalem in Judah to rebuild this Temple of the LORD ... And may your God be with you!

Ezra 1:2-3

After the Jewish people spent seventy years in captivity, God used a Persian king who wasn't serving God to return the Jews to their homeland. Cyrus even protected them, giving them money and materials to rebuild God's temple!

In a situation that looked impossible from a human standpoint, God intervened and used the heart of a foreign king to move the Jewish people where He wanted them to be. God has worked that way through all of history, and He works that way today.

What situation in your life looks impossible to you? Be encouraged by Proverbs 21:1, "The king's heart is like a stream of water directed by the LORD; He guides it wherever He pleases."

Father,
We rest in the promise that You are always guiding and directing us in the events of our lives. Amen.

October 9

Not by Your Bootstraps

The message of the cross is foolish to those
who are headed for destruction! But we who
are being saved know it is the very power of God.
1 Corinthians 1:18

"Pull yourself up by your bootstraps" is an idiom describing people who think they can solve a difficult problem themselves. From sports to business to motivational thinkers, variations on this theme abound.

While every culture has its own adaptations on this idiom, the idea is that we are on our own, and we must make it on our own. Christianity is unique among the world's religions, teaching that we can be saved only through the power of God.

That idea seems foolish to some in the world who think they need to earn their own way. But it is only the work that Jesus did on the cross that saves us, not our own efforts. Those who trust Him receive His power.

Lord,
Thank You that You have not left us on our own to solve our deepest problems. You alone are our salvation. Amen.

October 10

Does God Care?

He has not ignored or belittled the suffering
of the needy. He has not turned His back on them,
but has listened to their cries for help.

Psalm 22:24

There have been a few times in my life when I questioned whether God really cares about me. Grievous circumstances sometimes prompt such feelings.

After wallowing for a while, I thought, *Who else could I go to for wisdom, comfort, and guidance? Where else would I turn?* Then, I looked at God's Word.

He didn't ignore Hannah, I noticed. *He listened to the cries of the Psalmists. He delivered Daniel out of the lions' den. Since He was faithful to them, I will trust Him with my life too.*

If you are questioning whether God cares for you, hold on to the faith of those who have gone before you. Our doubts and questions don't make God any less faithful.

October 11

Father,
We are grateful for examples of Your faithfulness in other people's lives. We want to trust You, too. Amen.

The First Step

The whole remnant of God's people began to obey the
*message from the L*ORD *their God ... So the L*ORD *sparked*
the enthusiasm of Zerubbabel ... and ... Jeshua ... and
the enthusiasm of the whole remnant of God's people.
They began rebuilding the house of their God.

Haggai 1:12, 14

Obedience to God begins with a first step. In the
short Old Testament book of Haggai, the main message was "Rebuild the Temple!"

For sixteen years, the remnant of Jewish people
who had returned from Palestine had left the work
undone. The prophet Haggai exhorted the people
to get to work!

When they took the first step, God blessed them.
He inspired their hearts with enthusiasm to keep
going.

Is there an area of obedience to God in your life
that has been sitting idle? Begin to obey today,
and watch for God to spark your enthusiasm and
bless you.

Father,
Sometimes we're slow to obey. Give us strength to take the first
step, and enthusiasm to keep going. Amen.

October 12

Building the Church

Because of God's grace to me, I have laid the foundation
like an expert builder. Now others are building on it.
But whoever is building on this foundation must
be very careful. For no one can lay any foundation
other than the one we already have – Jesus Christ.

1 Corinthians 3:10-11

St. Paul's Cathedral towers over central London. Designed by Sir Christopher Wren, the present cathedral was begun in 1675 and took thirty-five years to build. Prior to this, three other churches dedicated to St. Paul occupied the site, dating back to A. D. 604.

St. Paul's Cathedral is built on the foundation of the earlier churches, but Paul himself reminds us that church is not a mere physical structure, but rather the people of Christ.

Just as a great cathedral must be carefully built on a solid foundation, so we must be careful that our lives point to Christ, the sure foundation. He is the One on whom we build.

Lord,
May our thoughts, words, and actions be built on You. Amen.

October 13

Mutter, Mutter, Mutter

*The very next morning the whole community of Israel
began muttering against Moses and Aaron.*
Numbers 16:41

One sad event of the Israelites' journey through the wilderness was the rebellion of Korah. Refusing to be content with the job he had, Korah grabbed for more power, criticizing Moses' leadership in the process.

Korah, and the people who went along with him, ended up losing their lives for their rebellion. Surprisingly, the very next morning the community was muttering ... again. For their rebellion, almost 15,000 died.

History is an excellent teacher. Small seeds of discontent that progress to complaining and sarcasm often end up in open hostility against God. With the help of God's Spirit and God's strength, we can avoid falling into the pit of discontent.

God,
As Your truth shines into our hearts, please help us to see our discontent for what it is. Strengthened by Your grace, enable us to deal with discontent swiftly and decisively. Amen.

October 14

Growing Roots

*Now, just as you accepted Christ Jesus as your Lord,
you must continue to follow Him. Let your roots grow
down into Him, and let your lives be built on Him.
Then your faith will grow strong in the truth you were
taught, and you will overflow with thankfulness.*

Colossians 2:6-7

In his letter to the Colossians, Paul described the process of growing in faith as letting our roots grow down into Christ. Roots anchor a plant, absorbing water and nutrients, and storing sugars and carbohydrates the plant needs in order to grow.

Following Christ – letting our roots grow down into Him – does the same thing. As we get to know God through spending time in His Word, several things happen. We become anchored. We know the truth and we aren't tossed around indecisively.

Absorbing nutrients from God's Word, our roots grow down and we grow up. We store up God's wisdom and knowledge. We're equipped for the varied challenges of life. What kind of nutrients are our roots absorbing?

Father,
May we grow strong by spending time in Your Word. Amen.

October 15

Be a Star

*Those who are wise will shine as bright as the sky,
and those who lead many to righteousness
will shine like the stars forever.*

Daniel 12:3

Each morning when I read the newspaper, I see pictures of stars. Movie stars. Rock stars. Sports stars. Apparently, people are fascinated with stars. We're intrigued with people who work under the bright lights of movie shoots, rock concerts, and sports events.

The Bible describes a different kind of star – a star that lasts forever. People who follow God – who live wisely and lead others to the righteousness that's found in Christ – are bright lights.

John the Baptist is a good example. In John 5:35, Jesus described him as a "burning and shining lamp." We can be one of God's stars, too, by pointing others to Christ.

Father,
Please help us to look for stardom in the right way – to shine brightly for You. Amen.

October 16

Avoid Drifting

So we must listen very carefully to the truth
we have heard, or we may drift away from it.
Hebrews 2:1

On December 23, 2006, two scuba divers who had been drifting for four hours were found off the coast of New South Wales, Australia. They were found by a merchant ship after the anchor line on their boat snapped. Their boat had drifted away from the Brooms Head area where they'd been diving.

Drifting isn't a hazard only at sea. It can happen with our hearts, too. If we're not steadily anchored to God's truth, we'll find ourselves straying and wandering, causing all sorts of problems to ourselves, our families, and our communities.

Staying anchored to God's Word now helps us avoid being picked up by a "Search and Rescue Squad" later.

Father,
We don't want to drift from Your truth. We're grateful that Your Word charts a safe path. Amen.

October 17

Relationship, Not Rituals

*Solomon, my son, learn to know the God
of your ancestors intimately. Worship and serve Him
with your whole heart and a willing mind. For the LORD
sees every heart and knows every plan and thought.
If you seek Him, you will find Him.*

1 Chronicles 28:9

In a dramatic ceremony, King David summoned all the officials of Israel to Jerusalem. He wanted them to be witnesses at the commissioning of his son, Solomon, to build the temple.

David began addressing the crowd by summarizing God's work, both in his life and in the life of the nation. He then handed the temple plans over to Solomon with the solemn charge to take the work seriously.

Of the many things David might have said to Solomon, he urged him to seek God and to know Him intimately. His words continue to help us today, when it remains possible to fall into meaningless rituals instead of pursuing a rich relationship with God.

Lord,
Sometimes I get caught up in religious rituals. Help me to long for intimacy with You instead. Amen.

Lunch with the Lord

Mary sat at the Lord's feet, listening to what He taught. But Martha was distracted by the big dinner she was preparing. The LORD said to her, "My dear Martha ... There is only one thing worth being concerned about. Mary has discovered it."

Luke 10:39-42

Recently, my husband had lunch with a friend who is heavily involved in serving others. His friend described the sense of duty and weariness he felt being involved in so many people's lives.

He mentioned that if he were sitting across from Jesus having lunch, he would ask Him, "Why is this so hard? I thought You said Your burden is easy."

Like Martha, we sometimes live our Christian lives as a matter of duty and tasks. If we could sit with Jesus as Mary did, imagine the joy and peace we would experience in His care.

Jesus has said He is with us day by day, waiting for us to be with Him, listening for His words of encouragement and peace.

Lord,
Keep me from the drudgery of duty and please fill me with the joy of Your presence. Amen.

October 19

Bigger Than the Sea

"Have you explored the springs from which the seas come? Have you explored their depths?"

Job 38:16

My family enjoys vacationing at Orange Beach, Alabama. The sound of the surf, the rising of the tides, and the vastness of the water captivate us. More than 70 percent of the earth is covered by oceans. It is a stunning, mysterious frontier.

As Job was questioned by God, he began to see God's creative power and infinite wisdom. God not only had intimate knowledge of the sea and its depths, but He was its Creator.

Next time you walk along the shore of an ocean and gaze out over the water, remember that God knows you intimately and fully. He longs for you to come and worship Him in all His fullness.

Lord,
When we look out on the ocean, we are reminded of Your greatness. Please strengthen us and fill us with awe for You. Amen.

October 20

Get a Grip

*With all these things in mind, dear brothers and sisters,
stand firm and keep a strong grip on the teaching we
passed on to you both in person and by letter.*

2 Thessalonians 2:15

When you think of "standing firm," what pictures come to mind? A person refusing to compromise? A teacher unwilling to bend the rules? A parent standing up for her kids?

Have you ever questioned whether someone's dogmatic viewpoint was really true? Paul was concerned about the evil influence of false teachers slipping into the church and confusing the believers about the coming of the Lord.

Having an open mind to what we need to learn is essential, but we must also have a strong grip on the essentials. The more we know of the Bible, the better equipped we will be to discern between truth and error. It must be the measure for our faith and actions.

Lord,
Thank You that You have given us Your word in the Bible. Help us to be diligent in its study, and persistent in gripping its truths. Amen.

October 21

Hope in Abandonment

Even if my father and mother abandon me,
the LORD will hold me close.
Psalm 27:10

When people are abandoned, not only are they left alone, but they're also left with a lot of pain. Some live with a family member who walks out of the room (literally or figuratively) whenever things get tense. Others feel abandoned because a parent or spouse spends unhealthy amounts of time or money on things like alcohol or work, neglecting their relationships.

The ultimate abandonment, sadly, is felt by some whose parents or spouses have totally left them behind. I'm grateful that God offers hope and comfort for such situations. He promises to embrace, hang on to, keep close, and nourish those who've been abandoned by others.

The pain of abandonment will still surface at times, but God's love outlasts the pain.

Father,
Thank You that Jesus endured the pain of abandonment on the cross, so that we wouldn't have to endure eternal separation from You. Amen.

October 22

A Lost Coin

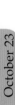

*"Suppose a woman has ten silver coins and loses one ...
when she finds it, she will call in her friends and
neighbors and say, 'Rejoice with me because I have
found my lost coin.' In the same way, there is joy in the
presence of God's angels when even one sinner repents."*

Luke 15:8-10

The silver coins the woman received had probably
been given as a traditional wedding gift, and therefore had enormous sentimental value. They would
be treasured in the same way a woman today values
her engagement ring.

On three different occasions, my mother discovered that the diamond from her engagement ring
had disappeared from the setting. On each occasion,
she was able to find it. Oh, her great happiness!

Jesus told the parable of the lost coin to illustrate
that God places great value on lost people. He
reminds us that there is great joy in heaven when
even one person returns to His love.

Lord,
Help me to remember that in Your eyes, I have inestimable
worth. Thank You for sending Jesus to redeem me. Amen.

October 23

Enduring Fame

Your name, O LORD, endures forever;
Your fame, O LORD, is known to every generation.
Psalm 135:13

Think about famous people from history. What names spring to your mind? Aristotle? An ancient Greek philosopher who lived from 384 B. C. to 322 B. C. – he's been famous for approximately eighty generations. Michaelangelo? An Italian Renaissance artist who lived from 1475-1564, he's been famous for about seventeen generations. George Washington? The first President of the United States who lived from 1732-1799, he's been famous for about nine generations.

The fame of these men has continued for many years, but it hasn't been known to every generation. Only God qualifies for that kind of fame.

Although we could never experience relationships with Aristotle, Michaelangelo or George Washington, we can have a relationship with God, whose fame continues to be known for all generations.

Father,
We're grateful that we can have a close relationship with a real celebrity. Amen.

October 24

Citizens of Heaven

Above all, you must live as citizens of heaven,
conducting yourselves in a manner worthy
of the Good News about Christ.
Philippians 1:27

We are citizens of heaven, where the Lord Jesus Christ lives.
And we are eagerly waiting for Him to return as our Savior.
Philippians 3:20

As I have traveled internationally, I've been reminded that citizenship is important. Whether entering Brazil, Bahamas, Germany, or the Virgin Islands, I've needed proof that I'm a U. S. citizen.

The apostle Paul explains that when we trust Christ, we become citizens of heaven, where we will settle some day.

When Christ returns to take us there, our passport will not be a document that we pay for or secure by our own efforts. Our passport to citizenship in heaven is our faith in Christ. If we confess Christ on earth, He confesses our names in heaven, where our names are written down – forever.

Father,
We're grateful that our citizenship in heaven doesn't depend on a human document, but on faith in Christ. Amen.

October 25

A Never-Ending Dynasty

"And now, may it please You to bless the house of Your servant, so that it may continue forever before You. For You have spoken, and when You grant a blessing to Your servant, O Sovereign Lord, it is an eternal blessing!"

2 Samuel 7:29

The book of second Samuel records the life of the greatest king of Israel – David. God spoke through the prophet Nathan about the blessing He would give to David, a blessing of an eternal dynasty. Generations of David's descendants would reign after him.

To a middle-Eastern monarch, no blessing could have been more profound. Looking at history, though, one might wonder if God kept His promise – the Jews were deported, the kingdom lost, and centuries of Jewish people were dispersed across the face of the earth.

God's promise has been kept – in Jesus Christ. As a descendant of David, He is the One who fulfills God's promise of an eternal reign. He is the Son of God, the King of kings, and His rule shall never end.

Lord Jesus Christ,
Thank You that You always keep Your word. Amen.

October 26

In God We Trust

Perseverance must finish its work so that you may be mature and complete, not lacking anything.
James 1:4 (NIV)

The United States Mint released a series of $1 coins honoring four presidents. The mint released more than 300 million of the gold colored coins before they discovered a problem. Words that were to have been engraved around the edge of the coins were missing, including, "In God We Trust, *E Pluribus Unum*," and the date and mint marks.

Sometimes we feel as though we're missing something in our Christian experience. It may be a lack of passion, the capacity to endure our circumstances, or difficulty managing our emotions. The good news is that when we place our trust in God, we can be assured that we will not lack anything in the end. By perseverance, God will finally cause us to be a "proof set" of His grace.

October 27

Lord,
We may be in various phases of "manufacturing," but in the end Your perfect plan will be completed in us. Give us the grace to persevere and allow You to mature us. In Jesus' name. Amen.

Extending Mercy

But Joseph replied, "Don't be afraid of me. Am I God, that I can punish you? You intended to harm me, but God intended it all for good. He brought me to this position so I could save the lives of many people."
Genesis 50:19-20

Joseph's brothers were terribly cruel to him. Because of this, his brothers feared that Joseph might want to take revenge on them after their father died.

When the brothers asked for Joseph's forgiveness – although in a manipulative way – Joseph responded that it was not his responsibility to punish them. Joseph left that to God, and extended forgiveness to his brothers.

Forgiving a person does not mean that we protect them from the painful consequences of their selfishness. But it does mean that we don't attempt to even the score by putting that person at a disadvantage. We leave justice and revenge to God, extending mercy to others because God has extended mercy to us.

Father,
We're grateful for Your mercy to us. Please help us extend Your mercy to others. Amen.

October 28

How Long Is a Day?

*A day is like a thousand years to the Lord, and
a thousand years is like a day. The Lord isn't really
being slow about His promise, as some people think.
No, He is being patient for your sake. He does not want
anyone to be destroyed, but wants everyone to repent.*

2 Peter 3:8-9

Most of us think of a day as 24 hours – the time it takes the earth to revolve around the sun. Actually, it takes 23 hours and 56 minutes – not quite a day.

There's a whole world of scientific study on the keeping of time, making highly calculated clock adjustments to keep track of what we commonly know as "a day."

Thankfully, God does not get confused by all these seemingly imprecise variables, nor does He live within the confines of what we call "Coordinated Universal Time." God is never early or late, fast or slow. He is patient as He waits for us to turn to Him.

Lord,
Thank You that You thought of us before time began and long for us to turn to You. Amen.

Close to the Humble

*Though the LORD is great, He cares for the humble,
but He keeps His distance from the proud.*

Psalm 138:6

There are things we like to stay close to – like water, food, and beloved family. There are things we'd rather keep a distance from – like fire, plagues, and poison.

The Bible describes the type of people that God keeps close to – the humble. He stays near to people who are unassuming and unpretentious. He tends to them and watches over them. The Bible also describes the kind of people that God keeps His distance from – the proud.

Instead of being at the forefront of an arrogant and presumptuous person's life, God is on the horizon. He keeps a range of space between Himself and proud people. What a difference it would make in our lives and relationships if, each day, we humbled ourselves before God!

Father,
We confess that we frequently struggle with pride. We want to humble ourselves and experience Your care. Amen.

October 30

See What We Don't See

Faith is the confidence that what we hope for will actually happen; it gives us assurance about things we cannot see.

Hebrews 11:1

Which of the following two quotes reflects the way you usually think?
- "Faith is to believe what we do not see; and the reward of this faith is to see what we believe." – St. Augustine.
- "Seeing is believing" – Unknown source.

In some cases it is important to subscribe to the latter. We want to see goods or services offered before we blindly pay for something. But when it comes to matters of Christian faith, the Bible teaches us that faith is essential. In fact, without it we cannot please God.

The eleventh chapter of Hebrews goes on to detail the lives of many saints, all of whom pleased God precisely because they could not see what they hoped for. In God's economy, part of the reward will be our sight.

Lord,
Sometimes my faith is weak. Please strengthen it, and help me to live in the confidence of things I will someday see. Amen.

October 31

November

Preparations

"Look! I the Lord am sending My messenger,
and he will prepare the way before Me."
Malachi 3:1

Preparations matter. Whether we're putting together a lasagna dinner, planning a wedding reception, or cleaning the walls of a room before painting, preparations are important. They lay the groundwork for something yet to happen.

The Old Testament prophet Malachi foretold that John the Baptist would prepare the way for Jesus. John did his job so well that Jesus, speaking to the crowds about John the Baptist in Matthew 11:11 said, "Of all who have ever lived, none is greater than John the Baptist."

Today, we can offer thanks to God for people He used in our lives to prepare us for a relationship with Him. We can also ask God to help us share His Good News with others.

Father,
May we be faithful messengers of Your truth and grace.
Amen.

November 1

Stir it Up

For I know how eager you are to help, and I have been boasting to the churches in Macedonia that you in Greece were ready to send an offering a year ago. In fact, it was your enthusiasm that stirred up many of the Macedonian believers to begin giving.

2 Corinthians 9:2

Whenever I make cinnamon applesauce, I begin by stirring two teaspoons of cinnamon into 1½ cups of sugar. At first I think, *Not much is happening – I might be stirring for a while.* But with each successive scrape of the spoon, I see more shades of brown and fewer shades of white. Next, I pour one cup of water into the sugar mixture and stir again.

Finally, after peeling, coring, and slicing about 20 apples, I stir everything together and cook it in the crock pot on low for 8-10 hours. Has my enthusiasm for making applesauce stirred you to try the recipe? It was the church at Greece whose enthusiasm stirred the Macedonian believers to begin giving offerings. Enthusiasm can be stirring!

Father,
Please help us to stir one another towards building Your Kingdom. Amen.

November 2

Pray for Courage

"Be strong and courageous! Do not be afraid or discouraged.
For the LORD your God is with you wherever you go."

Joshua 1:9

Several years ago, a friend of mine from church was diagnosed with pancreatic cancer. Seated around a conference table with twelve other deaconesses at one of our meetings, I asked Marsha, "How can we pray for you?" I'll never forget her response. "Please pray," she said quietly, "that I would have courage." I sat there thinking, *What a mature thing to pray for.*

During the months between the day her cancer was diagnosed and the day she went to be with Jesus, Marsha's courage inspired the faith of God's people around her. At times when our hearts feel fearful, courage is an honest and wonderful thing to pray for. It's a gift God provides as we depend on Him.

God,
Thank You for Your faithfulness to Marsha and her family during extremely difficult days. Thanks for the courage that You granted her. Please grant us the courage that we need. Amen.

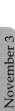

November 3

God's Children

See how very much our Father loves us, for He
calls us His children, and that is what we are!
I John 3:1

While teaching a piano lesson one afternoon, I noticed that eight-year-old David was wearing a silver chain around his neck. My curiosity got the best of me. "What's hanging on that cool silver chain?" I asked David. "My dad's dog tag!" he replied. David showed me the dog tag and went on to explain that his dad had served in the United States Air Force for several years.

The way he spoke about his father reflected a strong sense of identity and security – both signs of a well-loved child. God's children share the same benefits. When we place our faith in Christ, we become God's dearly loved children, gaining a new and growing sense of identity and security.

Loving Father,
Being Your children gives us security and identity. We are thankful. Amen.

November 4

Animals Wild and Fast

*God made all sorts of wild animals, livestock,
and small animals, each able to produce offspring
of the same kind. And God saw that it was good.*

Genesis 1:25

Of all the animals God has created, perhaps one of the most fascinating is the kangaroo. Native to Australia, it has become an icon of the country, even appearing on the tails of Australian airplanes. Kangaroos are the only large animals that hop as a means of locomotion. While a "roo" may typically travel about 13-16 mph (20-25 km/h), some have been known to reach speeds of 44 mph (70 km/h).

The kangaroo is a reminder of the vast, imaginative creation of God. God made all things large and small, and set them upon the earth to be observed and cared for by the crown of His Creation – man, created in His own image. "And God saw that it was good."

Lord,
What incredible diversity You built into Your Creation. Some animals frighten us, some fascinate us, and some make us laugh. Thank You for making so many things for us to enjoy!
Amen.

November 5

Clean Hearts

Create in me a clean heart, O God.
Renew a loyal spirit within me.
Psalm 51:10

One of my grandmas told me that she spoke the words of Psalm 51:10 out loud each morning: "Create in me a clean heart, O God. Renew a right spirit within me." What a great way to begin any day. Think of all the cleaning we do each day. We clean our teeth. We wash our faces. We lather our hands. We take a bath or a shower. We scrub pots and pans. We wipe off counters.

Our hearts need daily cleansing too. How gracious of God that He doesn't leave us on our own for that task. We could never do it ourselves. Through faith in His blood, He cleanses us and washes away our sin (1 John 1:7). Through His Word, He purifies us from the inside out (John 15:3).

God,
Thank You that Your shed blood gives us clean hearts through faith in Christ. Amen.

How to Pray?

We ask God to give you a complete knowledge of His will and to give you spiritual wisdom and understanding. Then the way you live will always honor and please the Lord, and your lives will produce every kind of good fruit.

Colossians 1:9-10

Do you sometimes feel baffled about how to pray for a friend or family member? You feel deep concern or you don't completely understand their situation, and you want to pray wisely. Praying God's Word is a wise and powerful thing to do. What better words can we speak to God on behalf of someone we care about than the words God spoke Himself?

While we ask God to make His will, wisdom, and understanding known to others, we're reminded that we want those things for ourselves too. It would be difficult to find a better prayer than to pray that we and those we love would honor God and produce good fruit.

Father,
Thank You for the truth of Your Word. Please plant it deep in our hearts so that we will know Your will and honor You. Amen.

November 7

When God Seems Distant

Search for the LORD and for His strength; continually seek Him. Remember the wonders He has performed, His miracles, and the rulings He has given, you children of His servant Abraham, you descendants of Jacob, His chosen ones.

Psalm 105:4-6

Do you ever think that God seems distant? Although it's not unusual for us to feel that way on occasion, it does feel unsettling. There is no instant cure for such feelings, but the psalmist suggests something helpful to do while we're waiting to feel closer to God. He suggests that we remember.

Remember God's wonders. We're to remember the miracles He did for other people in the past. Specifically, the psalmist mentions Abraham and Jacob, but there are plenty of other Bible characters to whom God demonstrated His wonders – Ruth, Daniel, Esther, Joseph, and Hannah, for starters. In the process of remembering what God has done for others in the past, our hearts are stirred to trust Him in the present.

Father,
Thank You for Your faithfulness to others in the past. We are encouraged to trust You now. Amen.

November 8

Dealing with Anger

And don't sin by letting anger control you.
Don't let the sun go down while you are still angry,
for anger gives a foothold to the devil.
Ephesians 4:26-27

Most people feel angry from time to time. That's not all bad. Anger can be a helpful signal, notifying us that something going on inside us or around us is unhealthy or unfair. Anger that's out of control, however, can cause plenty of destruction.

Lashing out thoughtlessly causes trouble, but so does bottling it up. So what do we do with our anger? Speaking the truth in love is a wise and healthy plan. It helps us express our feelings constructively, and reflects our feelings to a person who may need to hear how their words, attitudes, or behaviors are hurting us.

Dealing with anger in a healthy manner requires courage, but it's a God-honoring way to live.

Father,
It's a struggle to handle our feelings of anger properly. We long for Your help. Amen.

November 9

When You're Afraid

The Lord is my light and my salvation – so why should I be afraid? The Lord is my fortress, protecting me from danger, so why should I tremble?

Psalm 27:1

Everyone feels fear at one time or another – whether it's fear of failure, rejection, harm, or being exploited. How we deal with that fear is important. Left to itself, fear tends to become a black cloud, threatening to hold us captive.

David, the psalmist, presents us with a healthy way of attending to our fears. First, he recognizes that fear brings with it trembling, shivering, and shaking. David obviously understands! He also talks to himself about seeking God's presence and company. Then he asks God to help him through his fear, hide him in his time of fear, and deliver him from his fear.

By focusing on God, David shifts from fear to courageous confidence. We can, too.

Father,
Sometimes we are filled with fear. Please help us, hide us, and deliver us. In the powerful name of Jesus. Amen.

November 10

God Is Good

The LORD is good to those who depend on Him,
to those who search for Him. So it is good
to wait quietly for salvation from the LORD.
Lamentations 3:25-26

Whether we're waiting for a house to sell, a child to finish cancer treatment, or a relationship to improve, waiting is wearisome. The perspective we take determines whether we wait with dread or hope, worry or trust. God suggests something to do while we're waiting: search for Him.

Scouring His Word to see how He has been faithful to others in the past helps us in several ways. It gets our eyes off ourselves and on to God. It also promises us something ahead that's better than this life here on earth. When we see how He has been good to others, we're inspired to depend on His goodness to us too.

Father,
May we wait patiently for You and experience Your goodness.
Amen.

November 11

Facing a Crisis

"[Jesus] went on a little farther and fell to the ground. He prayed that, if it were possible, the awful hour awaiting Him might pass Him by. "Abba, Father," He cried out, "everything is possible for You. Please take this cup of suffering away from Me. Yet I want Your will to be done, not Mine."

Mark 14:35-36

How do we get through a crisis like cancer treatment, marital strife, or job loss? Since the biggest crisis of all time was faced by Jesus, we're wise to observe how He handled it. When Jesus experienced the most agonizing suffering imaginable, He did three things.

He asked God to take away the suffering. He acknowledged that everything is possible with God. He relinquished Himself to God's control. It's reassuring that there's nothing unspiritual about asking God to take away our suffering. If He doesn't though, we submit to His control.

The reason we can have a relationship with God is because in His crisis, Jesus submitted to God's control.

Faithful Father,
Give us grace to be faithful like Jesus. Amen.

November 12

God Understands Everyone

*The Lord looks down from heaven and sees
the whole human race. From His throne He observes
all who live on the earth. He made their hearts,
so He understands everything they do.*

Psalm 33:13-15

According to the Brazilian edition of the *Guinness World Book of Records*, Ziad Youssef Fazah is the world's greatest living polyglot – he speaks, reads, and understands almost 60 different languages! Born in Liberia to Lebanese parents, Ziad moved back to Lebanon with his family, and by the time he was 17, he spoke 54 languages. Other than Arabic, French, and English, he taught himself all the other dialects.

It's difficult to imagine being fluent in that many languages, but even harder to imagine that out of six thousand known languages, God understands them all. Beyond understanding the words, God understands the hearts of every person who has ever lived.

Lord,
We're grateful that because You made us, You understand us.
Amen.

November 13

Two Masked Bandits

With them were all the various kinds of animals –
those approved for eating and for sacrifice and those
that were not – along with all the birds and the small ani-
mals that scurry along the ground. They entered the boat in
pairs, male and female, just as God had commanded Noah.

Genesis 7:8-9

My husband and I looked out our kitchen window to see two raccoons sporting their signature "bandit" masks. Upon hearing our voices, the coons looked up to see what the commotion was and reluctantly ambled off. The pair reminded me of the story of Noah, where God caused the animals to make their way to the ark for safety, two-by-two.

Why did these animals come to the ark? They were moved to follow their Creator, the Lord God. Sometimes animals have more common sense than humans. They instinctively follow their Creator's plan. But God has given humans a choice. We are made in His image and have the ability – by faith – to live in obedience to God.

Lord,
You have given me more than instinct to live by. Help me to faithfully follow Your plan for my life today. Amen.

November 14

Living Proof

We prove ourselves by our purity,
our understanding, our patience, our kindness,
by the Holy Spirit within us, and by our sincere love.

2 Corinthians 6:6

It's not difficult to prove the law of gravity. But what does it mean to prove ourselves? The apostle Paul suggests looking at several things. Purity – are our thoughts and actions growing free from contamination? Understanding – do we understand that God made us, we sinned, God provided Jesus to save us and that we need Him? Patience – even in difficult situations, are we depending on God's Spirit? Kindness – are we showing kindness to others? Sincere love – are we pursuing a bold, sincere love for others that hates what is evil and clings to what is good? (Rom. 12:9)

This side of heaven we aren't perfect, but God's presence in us will bear evidences of purity, understanding, patience, kindness, and sincere love.

Father,
We could never manufacture godly qualities on our own.
Thanks for the work of Your Spirit in our lives. Amen.

November 15

Arrangements

*Now the L*ORD* had arranged for a great fish
to swallow Jonah. And Jonah was inside the fish
for three days and three nights.*
Jonah 1:17

If we imagine what it might be like to arrange the
whole world – to make plans for every person who's
ever lived, to direct things in every country in the
world – we would be imagining part of what God
does. God has always arranged things, He's doing
it now, and He always will.

Back in the Old Testament book of Jonah, we
learn that God arranged for a great fish to swallow
Jonah. Of all the places in the sea that Jonah could
have gone overboard, God had a great fish ready in
precisely the right place at just the right time. If God
can make perfect arrangements for a disobedient
prophet, He can do it for us too.

Father,
Please help us to trust Your arrangements in our lives. Amen.

November 16

Reap Kindness

Your kindness will reward you,
but your cruelty will destroy you.
Proverbs 11:17

As children walking home from elementary school, my brother and I occasionally had some spats. One time when we felt particularly mad at each other, we shouted, "Everything that you say about me bounces right back to you!" At the time, we didn't realize how accurate that statement was. Whether we're kind or whether we're not, the words and actions we say or do towards another person do bounce back to us.

What do we want to come springing back at us – compassion, gentleness, and understanding, or cruelty, callousness, and harshness? If we show kindness to a friend or family member, we're not demonstrating it only to them. We'll also feel it ourselves. The types of seeds we sow create a perpetual harvest. What would we like to reap?

Father,
Please help us to think of the impact our words have on those around us. Amen.

November 17

In the Genes

By His divine power, God has given us everything
we need for living a godly life. We have received all of
this by coming to know Him, the one who called us to
Himself by means of His marvelous glory and excellence.

2 Peter 1:3

Whether our eyes are blue, green, or brown, their color was determined by some of the 20,000-25,000 genes God equipped us with at birth. Genes are like little bits of information, giving off instructions as to how our bodies will grow and develop. Half of the blueprint comes from a mother's side, and half from a father's side.

When we are born into God's family through faith in Christ, we receive spiritual genes – everything we need for life and godliness. Our responsibility is not to go out looking for more spiritual genes. If we have a relationship with God, they're already there! As we spend time in the Bible and live in obedience to God, we will grow godly. It's in the genes.

Father,
Thank You that growth in godliness is not a mystery. Amen.

November 18

What Can You See?

The LORD doesn't see things the way you see them.
People judge by outward appearance,
but the LORD looks at the heart.

1 Samuel 16:7

Some years ago my husband had a major bicycle accident in which he broke his wrist and his jaw, each in three places. When I met him at the hospital, the breaks were obvious, but it took several X-rays to determine the extent of the damage. Thankfully, medical personnel have harnessed X-rays to observe and analyze the inside of our bodies.

People's secret behavior and motives, though, are more difficult to see and analyze. Sometimes we're unaware of what is really going on in someone's life. God does not need any special equipment to know these things. The Good News of the gospel is that in spite of God's awareness of our sin, He accepts us into His family through faith in Christ.

Lord,
We're grateful that You see things as they really are. Amen.

November 19

Loving Strength

The best-equipped army cannot save a king, nor is
great strength enough to save a warrior. Don't count
on your warhorse to give you victory – for all its strength,
it cannot save you. But the LORD watches over those who
fear Him, those who rely on His unfailing love.
Psalm 33:16-18

If you gathered all the troops from the armies of the United States, China, Israel, Russia, and India, there would be more than enough power to protect a group of people for some years to come. There would never be enough power, though, to prevent the eventual physical death of anyone on the earth, no matter how important or famous they may be.

Armies can protect people and keep them safe temporarily, but all of us will die at some point. God reminds us that He never intended for us to put our hope in military might – or money or medicare, for that matter. He wants us to place our hope in Him. In God, we find salvation and unfailing love that last forever.

Lord,
Nowhere else is there such a combination of strength and love as there is in You. We praise You. Amen.

November 20

Gift of Prayer

I urge you, first of all, to pray for all people. Ask God to help
them, intercede on their behalf, and give thanks for them.
1 Timothy 2:1

I appreciated the unusual gift that my friend Ruthie
gave me, because it came at a time I was discouraged.
"While I was raking leaves the other day," Ruthie
said, "I spent half an hour praying for you." Thirty
minutes for me? Wow! I pray for family and friends
each day, but I don't usually devote half an hour to
each person.

God urges us, though, to pray for one another.
In 1 Timothy 2:1, He elaborates how. *Ask for God's*
help. That's where we get the words "prayer re-
quest". *Intercede.* We communicate with God out of
concern for another person. *Give thanks.* We express
gratitude for what God has done, is doing, and will
do. Prayer doesn't come in a box, but it's a gift of
eternal value.

Father,
When we're concerned about a friend or family member, may
we give them the gift of prayer. Amen.

November 21

Special Possession

Moses immediately threw himself to the ground and worshiped. And he said, "Oh Lord, if it is true that I have found favor with You, then please travel with us. Yes, this is a stubborn and rebellious people, but please forgive our iniquity and our sins. Claim us as Your own special possession."

Exodus 34:8-9

After the Israelites sinned by worshiping the golden calf they made, God was ready to destroy them all. But Moses pleaded with God and He relented. There was punishment for their sin, but He demonstrated Himself to be full of mercy and forgiveness.

Moses' response to God's justice and mercy is a beautiful example for us. Moses worshiped, thanked God for His favor and asked God to travel with them. He acknowledged their tendency to sin, asked for God's forgiveness, and asked God to claim them as His own special possession. What a beautiful picture of the restored relationship with God that we can experience when we repent of sin in our hearts.

Father,
We're grateful for the gift of Your forgiveness. May we see ourselves as Your special possession. Amen.

November 22

Light and Truth

Send out Your light and Your truth;
let them guide me. Let them lead me to Your
holy mountain, to the place where You live.
Psalm 43:3

The psalmist's heart was obviously troubled. *Why have you tossed me aside? Why must I wander around in grief? Why am I being oppressed by my enemies?* It's helpful for us to listen in on his feelings, because there are times when we ask such questions too.

For a moment, we wonder if the psalmist decided to turn away from God. But he ran toward God and asked Him to send a couple of escorts for the journey! He asked for light, because he was having trouble finding his way, and truth, because he needed guidance from someone who saw the whole picture. God still delivers His light and truth to us when we ask Him for guidance today.

God,
We need Your escorts of light and truth for our journey, too.
Amen.

Leaders Serve

*He sat down, called the twelve disciples over to Him,
and said, "Whoever wants to be first must take
last place and be the servant of everyone else."*
Mark 9:35

Jesus had been investing heavily in His disciples,
giving them large amounts of teaching, time, and
energy. When He ascended to heaven after His
death and resurrection, these disciples would be the
human leaders of His Kingdom on earth. Instead of
the disciples exhibiting proper leadership, though,
they were arguing over who was the greatest! Jesus
sat them down to have a little "talk."

He explained that in His Kingdom, leaders
don't *use* people to get to the top. Rather, they *serve*
people, realizing that no job is too small. In your
areas of leadership today – in the family as a parent,
at school as a teacher, or at work as an executive –
how might you lead by serving? Godly leadership
serves others.

Father,
We often get things mixed up, seeking recognition instead
of service. We repent and ask for Your grace to serve others.
Amen.

November 24

Gentle Trees and Grass

*A mighty windstorm hit the mountain … but the
L<small>ORD</small> was not in the wind … but the L<small>ORD</small> was not
in the earthquake … but the L<small>ORD</small> was not in the fire.
And after the fire there was the sound of a gentle whisper.*
1 Kings 19:11-12

We have all heard stories of people who experienced a dramatic change in their lives. Perhaps we feel
disappointed that God has not worked that way
in our lives, or we long for a remarkable spiritual
experience. A friend of mine once observed that
God demonstrates His power through thunder and
lightning, but also through trees and grass.

The power demonstrated in a thunderstorm is
obvious, but we sometimes overlook the quiet
growth of trees and grass. When God rained down
fire before the priests of Baal, Elijah observed God's
power in a spectacular way. Later, when Elijah was
weary, afraid, and on the run, God came to him in
a gentle whisper. Sometimes, God's voice thunders.
Sometimes He whispers. Are we listening?

Lord,
Help me to remember that You are always working, whether it
is obvious or subtle. Either way, Your way is best. Amen.

November 25

What God Desires

"Make thankfulness Your sacrifice to God, and keep the vows You made to the Most High. Then call on Me when you are in trouble, and I will rescue you, and you will give Me glory."

Psalm 50:14-15

What does the God who made us ask of us? First, He desires our thanks. God was pleased with the sacrifices the Israelites were bringing to Him, but He already owned all the animals in the forest and on the hills. He really wanted their thanks.

Next, He asks us to obey Him. Obedience isn't a matter of ritualism or legalism – it's about living that springs from a heart devoted to God. Finally, God reminds us that He loves to hear and answer our prayers. Our dependence on Him displays His glory to those around us. What offerings of thanks, obedience, and dependence on God might you offer today?

God,
Thank You that what You desire from us isn't out of our reach. Your desire for us begins with our hearts. Amen.

November 26

Pray about Everything

Don't worry about anything; instead, pray about everything. Tell God what you need, and thank Him for all He has done. Then you will experience God's peace, which exceeds anything we can understand.
Philippians 4:6-7

The verse is straightforward – "Don't worry about anything; instead, pray about everything." We tend to get those words switched around. Sometimes we approach stressful days by worrying about everything and not praying about anything! I'm thankful that when Paul gave us this warning, he didn't stop with "Don't worry." Without something to replace my worry, I'd have difficulty moving away from it.

But Paul follows with some helpful words: "Pray about everything." *Everything* means the whole of our lives – every little thing! When we pray about everything, we'll experience God's peace that will guard our hearts and minds. So, "Don't worry about anything; instead, pray about everything."

November 27

Father,
We want to pray more and experience Your wonderful peace.
Amen.

God Remembers

*But God remembered Noah and all the
wild animals and livestock with him in the boat.*
Genesis 8:1

Whether it's making the insurance payment, sending a birthday card, or changing the furnace filter, all of us have things we need to remember. On occasions when we forget, we may feel embarrassed, but we realize that all human beings forget things from time to time. God, however, is different.

He always remembers. He has never forgotten to raise the sun in the morning or set it in the evening. He has never forgotten to bring on winter, spring, summer, or fall. God remembered Noah, just as He remembered Abraham, Joseph, David and the prophets. It is fitting for us to place our faith in God, because He remembers.

Father,
When we're tempted to think that You have forgotten us,
thanks for reminding us that You remember. Amen.

November 28

God Carries Us

"I have cared for you since you were born. Yes, I carried you before you were born. I will be your God throughout your lifetime — until your hair is white with age. I made you, and I will care for you. I will carry you along and save you."

Isaiah 46:3-4

While sightseeing in Koln, Germany, my husband and I climbed the five hundred steps to the top of the famous cathedral in the city. While resting at the highest point to catch our breath, we watched a father arrive at the top with a toddler in his arms. The father had done the climbing while the child enjoyed the ride.

We were warmed by the love and care of the father toward the child. As an adult, I don't feel the need to be carried anywhere physically, but I do need to be carried along spiritually and emotionally. I'm grateful that the God who carried me before I was born is still willing to carry me now.

Father God,
We praise You for Your willingness to care for us. Amen.

November 29

Access to God

*"Now you are My friends, since I have
told you everything the Father told Me."*
John 15:15
*So let us come boldly to the throne of our
gracious God. There we will receive His mercy,
and we will find grace to help us when we need it.*
Hebrews 4:16

Imagine that the president of your country sent you a personal letter informing you that you could spend as many hours, lunches, or visits with him as you wanted. How would you respond? Would you take him up on his invitation, or disregard it?

God wants to have a relationship with us, and He wants us to be His friends. How are we responding to His overtures? J. Oswald Sanders once said, "Each of us is as close to God as we choose to be." God – the Creator and Redeemer of the world – has issued us an open invitation to spend time with Him. How close do we want to be?

Father,
We're grateful that You want us to be Your friends. Thank You that because of Jesus' work on the cross, we can have open access to You. Amen.

November 30

December

A Ray of Hope

"For I know the plans I have for you," says the LORD.
"They are plans for good and not for disaster,
to give you a future and a hope."
Jeremiah 29:11

Most of us are acquainted with people who live with great difficulties; a marriage experiencing the deep wounds of betrayal, parents who have buried a child. Even people strong in faith experience days of gloominess when they struggle to find even a glimmer of hope.

The Old Testament prophet, Jeremiah, understood gloominess. He was part of a community that had been brutally dragged off more than 700 miles from their home in Jerusalem. Many had seen friends or relatives killed and had no hope of seeing their homes again. In the midst of this deep despair, God broke through with rays of hopeful light. He had good plans for them. Jeremiah's words still encourage people today. God has good plans for us.

Lord,
Some days are very dark. When the future seems bleak, help us to see a ray of hope and understand that You have good plans for our lives. Amen.

December 1

Close to Christ

"Remain in Me, and I will remain in you. For a branch cannot produce fruit if it is severed from the vine, and you cannot be fruitful unless you remain in Me."

John 15:4

The word *remain* (abide; continue) is used by John eleven times in John 15! Staying in close relationship to Christ produces love, joy, patience, kindness, goodness, faithfulness, gentleness and self-control in us. These things bring glory to God and show Christ's love to others.

How do we remain, abide, or continue in Christ? By choosing to read the Bible, worship God, pray, confess our sins, and obey God because we love Him. These things do not come automatically. They need to be cultivated. Once we have seen and tasted the fruit that remaining in Christ produces, we won't want to live any other way.

Father,
We long for close relationships. Thank You that You want to be close to us. Amen.

December 2

The Mighty Tower

*From the ends of the earth, I cry to You for help
when my heart is overwhelmed. Lead me to the
towering rock of safety, for You are my safe refuge,
a fortress where my enemies cannot reach me.*

Psalm 61:2-3

One of the world's most popular tourist destinations is the Tower of London. Begun by William the Conqueror in 1078, it is actually a collection of fortress buildings surrounded by two security rings and a moat.

The tower has functioned as a fortress, a royal palace, and a prison. It has also been a zoo, a mint, an armory and has housed the Crown Jewels since 1303.

Throughout the course of history, people have sought to guard earthly possessions in the supposed safety of fortresses. God offers us the ultimate in safety – a fortress for our souls. Only He can truly protect us from the enemies of life, be they circumstances or people.

Lord,
The circumstances of my human safety may change, but You,
Lord, never change. You are my fortress! Amen.

December 3

Overcome with Encouragement

*I am certain that God, who began the good work
within you will continue His work until it is finally
finished on the day when Christ Jesus returns.*

Philippians 1:6

The words above encouraged me at a very dark time of my life. Overcome with sadness and a sense of hopelessness, I was struggling to keep going. While driving on the expressway one afternoon, I heard a vocalist on the radio singing the words of Philippians 1:6.

I was so overcome with emotion that I moved my car off the expressway and stopped on the side of the road. There were too many tears to keep driving. I felt incredibly encouraged to think that God doesn't give up on me or on those I love! The work that He begins in our hearts when we trust Him is a work that He continues until He comes again.

God,
Thank You for the good work You began in me. Thank You for continuing that good work. Amen.

December 4

Celebrate

Praise the LORD, for the LORD is good;
celebrate His lovely name with music.
Psalm 135:3

If you enjoy festive occasions, here's some good news. God's Kingdom is all about celebrating – celebrating God and His goodness to us. In spite of the fact that we humans sometimes rebel against God, He still pursues us. That is something to celebrate. We can celebrate in the morning, thanking God that we are alive.

At lunch, we can celebrate His generosity in providing our meal of turkey and cheddar cheese on rye bread. In the evening, we can celebrate by thanking Him for minds able to recall and process the varied events and exchanges of the day. Most importantly, we can celebrate the gift of forgiveness God provided through Jesus Christ. That is something we will celebrate for all eternity.

Lord,
We want to celebrate You more often. Amen.

Holding Things Together

[Christ] existed before anything else,
and He holds all creation together.
Colossians 1:17

If you logged on to the Internet and typed in the question, "What holds the world together?" you'd find some interesting answers. Among the more humorous are duct tape and bamboo. A famous quote by former U. S. President Woodrow Wilson offers a different perspective. "Friendship," he said, "is the only cement that will hold the world together." Scientists say that fundamental particles we are reacting with hold the world together.

The Bible records that Christ holds all Creation together. He existed before anything else. He created everything. He is the goal of all Creation, and He holds it all together. Since Christ has done all of that, we can surely trust Him with our lives, our families, and our problems.

Father,
How could we face another day with confident trust if we didn't know that You hold all things together? Amen.

December 6

Seek Advisers

Without wise leadership, a nation falls;
there is safety in having many advisers.
Proverbs 11:14

Whether we're wrestling with problems in our personal lives, our jobs, or our relationships, seeking the counsel and advice of others is an intelligent thing to do. In fact, the Bible goes so far as to say that when we don't seek wise leadership, we're susceptible to stumbling, collapsing, or relapsing. How do we find wise leadership? Keep an eye out for people who are sensible, perceptive, and discreet.

Sometimes we learn just by watching. Other times, when we need more specific help, we can ask a wise person if he or she is willing to share skill, foresight, or guidance with us. Seeking wise people to coach us and make discerning recommendations offers us protection and a fresh perspective. We benefit greatly when we do.

Father,
It takes courage and humility to seek out advisers. Please help us to look for them sooner rather than later. Amen.

December 7

Message for Everyone

That night there were shepherds staying in the fields nearby, guarding their flocks of sheep. Suddenly, an angel of the Lord appeared among them. He said, "I bring you good news that will bring great joy to all people. The Savior – yes, the Messiah, the Lord – has been born today in Bethlehem."

Luke 2:8-11

Many people celebrate the birth of Christ by going to a candlelight service held in a church. It's interesting that when God sent an angel to announce Jesus' birth, He didn't send the angel to a church or a temple. God sent the angel to people who didn't even go to church! In that culture, shepherds didn't participate in the religious activities of their community – they weren't welcome.

But God has always come to the humble, and on this occasion, He chose the shepherds. The good news announced long ago is still good news today. No matter what our country, family history, religion, job, or educational background, the message that Jesus saves is for everyone.

Father,
Thank You that Your love transcends all human boundaries and reaches to everyone. Amen.

December 8

First Magnitude Spring

*Jesus replied, "Anyone who drinks this water will soon
become thirsty again. But those who drink the water I give
will never be thirsty again. It becomes a fresh, bubbling
spring within them, giving them eternal life."*

John 4:13-14

Bubbling up to the surface of the earth in Florida
are more than 33 fresh water springs. These "first
magnitude springs" have an output of more than
100 cubic feet of water per second! That's almost
750 gallons (about 2,850 liters) of water.

Water is what Jesus was looking for when He
wearily sat at a well and asked a thirsty woman for
a drink. Unknown to her, Jesus knew that her thirst
was not merely physical – it was also spiritual. At
the well Jesus offered her "living water" that would
bubble up from within her spirit, refreshing her and
those around her. He offers us that same crystal
clear refreshment of spirit. Take a drink!

Dear Jesus,
It is not wealth, status, possessions or anything else that
quenches the thirst I feel in life. Help me to turn nowhere else
but to You. Amen.

The Roar of Love

*I hear the tumult of the raging seas as Your waves
and surging tides sweep over me. But each day
the LORD pours His unfailing love upon me.*
Psalm 42:7-8

On a trip to Niagara Falls, my husband and son decided to hike along the boardwalk near the base of the falls. They noticed one particular vantage point marked "The Hurricane Deck." Smiling at the image this raised in their minds, they made that their destination. This was a windy deck at the base of the falls that came close to the rush of the nearly 750,000 gallons of water per second that roar over the falls.

Sometimes the circumstances of our lives make us feel as though we are being swamped by the violent waves of a hurricane. Thankfully, the psalmist reminds us of a more potent force than the crush of life – the unfailing love of God.

Lord God,
In the roar of life today, help me to remember that the seeming whisper of Your unfailing love is stronger than my life's circumstances. Amen.

December 10

In Royalty's Presence

Because of Christ and our faith in Him, we can
now come boldly and confidently into God's presence.
Ephesians 3:12

Ever since I wrote a report on Luxembourg back when I was in fourth grade, I've wanted to visit that tiny European country. Let's pretend for a moment that I received an invitation not only to visit Luxembourg but also to meet the Chief of State – Grand Duke Henri. That would be a little intimidating. Grand Duke Henri has no reason to be interested in me.

A relationship with God – the King of all heaven and earth – is totally different. He proved how much He cares about all of us when He gave His life for us. Because He is the One who secured our relationship with Him, we can come into His presence with confidence and certainty. We can have a relationship with Royalty!

Father,
May I come into Your presence often! Amen.

Tears in a Bottle

You keep track of all my sorrows.
You have collected all my tears in Your bottle.
You have recorded each one in Your book.

Psalm 56:8

One thing that I appreciate about my friends is that they care about me. It means a lot when my friends celebrate my joy and empathize with my sadness. At times when I'm sad enough to need a good cry, I feel comfortable letting go around close friends. I find huge encouragement, then, in discovering that God cares about my sorrows enough to collect and record my tears.

Since our eyes produce an average of 10 oz. of lubricating tears per day, God would need a good-sized bottle on days when we shed extra tears! To think that the God who made us and sustains us also collects and records our tears is astounding. He really cares about us.

Kind Father,
Thank You that You care about us. Amen.

December 12

Word Choices

*Don't use foul or abusive language. Let everything
you say be good and helpful, so that your words
will be an encouragement to those who hear them.*
Ephesians 4:29

When we first trust Christ and God's Spirit takes
up residence in our hearts, it's as though each of us
receives a personal speech therapist. God's Spirit is
in the practice of transforming hearts. He changes
words of cursing and bitterness into words that
benefit and encourage others.

"Change the heart," says Warren Wiersbe, "and
you change the speech." The more our hearts are
filled with the love of Christ, the more our words
will be good, helpful, and encouraging to the people
around us. When in doubt about what to say – and
some of us could use a few more doubts – maybe
it would be wise to ask ourselves, "Is it good? Is it
helpful? Is it encouraging?"

Father,
Words are powerful things. Please help us to choose words that
are good and helpful. Amen.

December 13

Shepherd of My Life

Then [Jacob] blessed Joseph and said, "May the God before whom my grandfather Abraham and my father, Isaac, walked – the God who has been my shepherd all my life, to this very day, the Angel who has redeemed me from all harm – may He bless these boys."

Genesis 48:15-16

Jacob, the Old Testament patriarch, spoke what I consider to be some of the most beautiful words in the Bible: "The God who has been my shepherd all my life ..." I identify with those words, because God is my faithful Shepherd too. Jacob's words offer special encouragement to anyone who has ever been a rebel or cares about a rebel.

When Jacob was young, he was a scheming and dishonest man. By God's grace, though, his life turned around. Despite a rocky start, Jacob eventually submitted to God's leadership and found God to be his faithful Shepherd for all of life. When we submit to God, we find Him to be our faithful Shepherd too.

Father,
Thank You for being a faithful Shepherd to us and to those we love. Amen.

December 14

God's Orchestrations

But you, O Bethlehem Ephrathah, are only a small village among all the people of Judah. Yet a ruler of Israel will come from you, one whose origins are from the distant past.
Micah 5:2
Jesus was born in Bethlehem.
Matthew 2:1

Although Ruth in the Old Testament was born in Moab, God moved her to Bethlehem. After she had just experienced the loss of her husband, moving must have seemed like a huge inconvenience. But God needed Ruth in Bethlehem. He planned for her to be the great grandmother of King David.

Years later, Mary and Joseph had to travel to Bethlehem for taxation purposes. Imagine traveling 80 miles on a donkey when Mary was about to give birth! But God was fulfilling Micah's prophecy and accomplishing yet another part of His plan for the world. The God who orchestrated events in the lives of Ruth, David, Mary and Joseph is the same God who orchestrates our lives today.

All-Knowing God,
Thank You that Your plans are good and that You are in control. Amen.

December 15

A Great House Guest

*When Jesus came by, He looked up at Zacchaeus
and called him by name. "Zacchaeus!" He said.
"Quick, come down! I must be a guest in your home today."
Zacchaeus quickly climbed down and took
Jesus to his house in great excitement and joy.*

Luke 19:5-6

Zacchaeus was known for two things: he was short, and he cheated. As a regional tax collector, he took opportunities to skim a little extra from his countrymen on their taxes, saving some for himself. Not surprisingly, Zacchaeus lived as a social outcast from Jewish society. Little did he know, though, that God Himself had taken note of him.

When Jesus, the Son of God, passed by a tree that Zacchaeus had climbed, Jesus called to Zacchaeus and announced that He wanted to visit in his home. The encounter changed Zacchaeus's life. Jesus has called us by name too. He comes to meet us in our circumstances, changing us from the inside out.

Lord,
Thank You that despite my shortcomings and failures, You have noticed me. Amen.

December 16

Don't Give Up

Our ancestors trusted in You, and You rescued them.
They cried out to You and were saved.
They trusted in You and were never disgraced.
Psalm 22:4-5

Do you ever struggle in prayer because you wonder if it really helps? Apparently David did, too. He opened Psalm 22 with, "My God, my God, why have You abandoned me? Why are You so far away when I groan for help? Every day I call to You, my God, but You do not answer."

After David expressed his feelings to God, he did two helpful things. He looked upward – he acknowledged God's holiness and sovereignty. He looked backward – he rehearsed times when his ancestors cried out to God and God rescued them. When we struggle in prayer, looking up to God and back in history, helps us too. When we trust in God, we will never be discouraged.

Father,
David's honesty is refreshing. Please help us never to give up trusting You. Amen.

December 17

A Reminder to Love

I am writing to remind you, dear friends, that we should love one another. This is not a new commandment, but one we have had from the beginning. Love means doing what God has commanded us, and He has commanded us to love one another, just as you heard from the beginning.

2 John 1:5-6

Sometimes we remind ourselves to pick up clothes from the cleaners, make a house payment, or make a hair appointment. Do we ever write ourselves a reminder to love? That's what the apostle John did in his second New Testament letter written from Ephesus. He prompted believers in Christ to love.

Love may include warm feelings, but the love we show one another is primarily an act of the will. It's even possible to act in love when we don't feel loving. We take our cues from God and treat people the way He has treated us – with patience, kindness, generosity, and compassion. John gave us a fresh reminder of an old commandment: LOVE.

Father,
We need Your help in loving one another. Amen.

December 18

Like a River

*The LORD will be our Mighty One. He will be like
a wide river of protection that no enemy can cross,
that no enemy ship can sail upon.*
Isaiah 33:21

Biblical writers used many images to describe God,
one of them being a river. Historically, large rivers
have provided protection to the cities around them.
Think, for example, of the Nile – the lifeline of the
ancient Egyptian civilization. Another of the largest
in the world is the Yangtze River in China. The
Chinese commonly say, "If you haven't traveled up
the mighty Yangtze, you haven't been anywhere!"

Even if you combined all the strength of the Nile,
the Yangtze, the Amazon, and the Rhine, it wouldn't
compare to the power of God. Almighty God has
power that is divine, unlimited, and unrestricted. It
is an awesome privilege to be in relationship with
the Lord, the Mighty One. When we are, we can
experience His unlimited power in our lives.

Mighty God,
We're grateful that we can live in relationship with You and
experience Your power personally. Amen.

December 19

Right Place, Right Time

*After the wise men were gone, an angel of the Lord
appeared to Joseph in a dream. "Get up! Flee to Egypt
with the child and His mother," the angel said.
"Stay there until I tell you to return, because Herod
is going to search for the child to kill Him."*
Matthew 2:13

I recently watched a movie titled *The Nativity*, and was reminded of God's complete control of history. During the volatile time surrounding Jesus' birth, there could have been any number of chances for something destructive to happen to Joseph, Mary, or Jesus. But God was preserving their young lives for special purposes.

He had them in just the right places at just the right times in order to bring us a Savior. Do you ever have moments when you wonder what on earth God is doing in your life? Remember how God cared for Mary, Joseph, and Jesus, and be inspired to believe that He will accomplish His purposes in your life, too.

Father,
You are in complete control. Help us to hold on to that even when things don't seem to make sense. Amen.

December 20

Death and Taxes

*"Now tell us – is it right for us to pay taxes to Caesar or
not?" He [Jesus] saw through their trickery and said, "Show
me a Roman coin. Whose picture and title are stamped on
it?" "Caesar's," they replied ... He said, "Give to Caesar what
belongs to Caesar, and give to God what belongs to God."*

Mark 12:15-17

It has been said, "The only sure thing in life is death
and taxes!" Most governments tax people to provide
for community services that citizens have come
to expect. Even though we sometimes pay taxes
begrudgingly, we would be unhappy if our roads
disappeared, or our airports suddenly closed!

While the power of a government might seem
overwhelming – sometimes even acting corruptly –
there is a higher authority to which each government
is responsible. In His great wisdom, Jesus affirmed
both the legitimacy of human government, and
its authority under the Kingdom of God. Both are
intended for our protection.

Sovereign God,
Give me the grace to respect those in authority over me,
realizing that all of Creation is accountable to You. Amen.

December 21

Fierce Love

*Because of the violence you did to your close relatives
in Israel, you will be filled with shame and destroyed
forever. When they were invaded, you stood aloof,
refusing to help them. Foreign invaders carried off
their wealth and cast lots to divide up Jerusalem,
but you acted like one of Israel's enemies.*
Obadiah 1:10-11

In order for us to understand what God was saying through the prophet Obadiah, we need a brief
update. Israel had descended from Jacob, while the
nation of Edom descended from Esau. The conflict
the two nations experienced in Obadiah's day can
be traced back to the birthright fiasco between Jacob
and Esau.

In Obadiah, God stood up to the Edomites like
a mother bear protecting her cubs. God's love for
His children was so fierce that He wouldn't overlook what was going on. When God's people are in
need, we must not stand aloof or gloat over prob-
lems.God is very protective of His children, and He
wants us to help them in their times of need.

Father,
May we always look out for and love Your children. Amen.

December 22

A River Runs through It

*Then the angel showed me a river with the water
of life, clear as crystal, flowing from the throne of God
and of the Lamb. It flowed down the center of the main
street. On each side of the river grew a tree of life, bearing
twelve crops of fruit, with a fresh crop each month.
The leaves were used for medicine to heal the nations.*
Revelation 22:1-2

The movie *A River Runs through It* chronicles the lives
of two brothers raised in a minister's home where
"there was no clear line between religion and fly
fishing." It is a story of relationships and struggles,
reminding us how fragile we all are.

In Revelation, we are told of another magnificent
river running through heaven. On its shores are
fruit trees that bring healing to those who have
encountered the difficulties of life, but have arrived
home by faith in Christ. There, life will not be about
fishing or religion, but about the presence of God
who will one day heal us from all of life's troubles.

Lord,
How we need Your healing! We look forward to seeing the
"crystal clear" river in our future home. Amen.

December 23

Shepherd and Lamb

*"I am the good shepherd. The good shepherd
sacrifices his life for the sheep."*
John 10:11

On the first Christmas Eve, the Good News of
Jesus' birth in Bethlehem was delivered by an
angel to shepherds tending their flocks outside
of Jerusalem. The flocks in their care were likely
sheep that were being raised to become sacrifices.
Sacrifices symbolized how much man owed God –
everything, because of sin. The sheep destined to
become animal sacrifices would eventually stand in
the place of people – an animal would die instead
of a person.

Isn't it curious, then, that the Good News about
Christ – the Good Shepherd who would sacrifice
His life for our sins – was announced to shepherds
who were tending sacrificial lambs? Christ became
both our Shepherd and our sacrificial Lamb!

Father God,
Because You gave Your life for us, we can trust You to lead us.
Amen.

December 24

Illuminating the Darkness

*"I have come as a light to shine in this dark world,
so that all who put their trust in Me will
no longer remain in the dark."*
John 12:46

I could gaze at Rembrandt's *The Adoration of the Shepherds* for a long time. The painting focuses on the infant Jesus, lying in a manger and illuminating an otherwise dark stable. One of the techniques Rembrandt used was chiaroscuro – making stark contrasts between light and darkness. He used the brightest part of the painting to illuminate the dark parts.

In this Nativity painting, the people whose faces reflect the most light are the people who are closest to Jesus. That's the way it works in real life, too. As we grow close to Jesus through faith, prayer, and time in God's Word, the darkness of sin dissipates while the light of Jesus is reflected in us.

Father,
Thank You that You bring light to our darkness. We want to stay close to You. Amen.

December 25

Faithful like Simeon

Simeon ... took [baby Jesus] in his arms and praised God, saying, "Sovereign Lord, now let Your servant die in peace, as You have promised. I have seen Your salvation, which You have prepared for all people. He is a light to reveal God to the nations, and He is the glory of Your people Israel!"
Luke 2:28-32

In a tiny amount of space, we learn a lot about a giant of a character. Simeon was righteous, devout, and eagerly waiting for the Messiah. He was full of God's Spirit, and God had promised him that he wouldn't die until he had seen Jesus. On the day that Mary and Joseph took the infant Jesus to the temple to be dedicated, God's Spirit led Simeon to the temple, where he spoke the beautiful blessing recorded above.

Simeon is a great role model for us. His life encourages us to see God as Sovereign and ourselves as God's servants. Through Simeon's experience, we're reminded that God keeps His promises, and that God's salvation is available to everyone.

Sovereign Lord,
May we be Your faithful servants, like Simeon. Amen.

Expectant Anna

*All these people died still believing what God had
promised them. They did not receive what was promised,
but they saw it all from a distance and welcomed it.*

Hebrews 11:13

*[Anna] came along just as Simeon was talking with
Mary and Joseph, and she began praising God.*

Luke 2:38

In a famous painting titled *Anna, the prophetess*,
Rembrandt captured the dignity of the old widow.
Sitting alone on a chair, Anna is reading a large
copy of the Scriptures, her right hand (pointing to
the words on the page) flooded with light.

Although this old woman with wrinkled and
thin skin wouldn't be considered attractive by society's standards, her beauty moved me to tears.
Anna was waiting for Jesus, the Redeemer, and God
allowed her to live long enough to see Him. I want
to love God's Word, be devoted to God, and have an
expectant heart like Anna.

Father,
Anna radiated her devotion to You. May I look expectantly for
You, too. Amen.

December 27

Bright Morning Star

A star will rise from Jacob.
Numbers 24:17
*Jesus was born in Bethlehem ... Wise men from
eastern lands arrived in Jerusalem, asking, "Where is the
newborn king of the Jews? We saw His star as it rose,
and we have come to worship Him."*
Matthew 2:1-2
"I am the bright morning star."
Revelation 22:16

Whether the star that led the wise men to Jesus was a temporary and supernatural light or a documented nova, we may not know until we get to heaven. But what we do know is that the star was prophesied in Numbers, fulfilled in Matthew, and wise men who traveled thousands of miles searching for Jesus found Him.

Because He is the only One in the world who can bring salvation to a seeking heart, those of us who search for Him will find Him to be our "Bright Morning Star."

Father,
We're grateful for the light that You bring to our lives. Amen.

December 28

Wiser Women

*These are the proverbs of Solomon, David's son,
king of Israel. Their purpose is to teach people wisdom and
discipline, to help them understand the insights of the wise.*

Proverbs 1:1-2

Spending time in Proverbs encourages us to do what is right, just and fair. The book teaches us wisdom and discipline, and helps us understand how wise people think. Imagine what might happen if we were to read one chapter of Proverbs every day of the year (Chapter 1 on January 1, Chapter 2 on January 2, etc.)

If we did that, we'd read each chapter of Proverbs twelve times in the course of one year. Or, if we chose to read two or three verses each day, we would read all the proverbs once in a year. If we're super ambitious, we could jump-start our desire to grow in wisdom by reading the whole book of Proverbs in one sitting. It only takes about 75 minutes – a great investment in wisdom and discipline.

Giver of Wisdom,
As we draw close to You through Your Word, we're grateful to become wiser women. Amen.

December 29

Tender Warnings

For no one is abandoned by the Lord forever.
Though He brings grief, He also shows compassion
because of the greatness of His unfailing love. For He
does not enjoy hurting people or causing them sorrow.
Lamentations 3:31-33

Imagine a loving mother who consistently warned her toddler not to touch the burners on the stove. The toddler, however, was bent on seeing what the burners were all about. He reasoned they couldn't be that bad. One day when the mom moved away from the stove to put a pan in the sink, the toddler dashed to the stove, touched the hot burner and seared his fingers.

We, as God's children, are sometimes like that toddler. If we don't take God's warnings seriously, we discover that sin brings sorrow and tragedy. In our pain, God doesn't stand idly by saying "I told you so!" Even when we experience the painful consequences of sin, He is full of compassion and loving-kindness. God has a tender heart towards His children.

Father, thank You for Your compassionate love. Amen.

December 30

Time to Account

"The master was full of praise. 'Well done, my good and faithful servant. You have been faithful in handling this small amount, so now I will give you many more responsibilities. Let's celebrate together!'"
Matthew 25:21

Many people dread accounting classes! The details of all the concepts and what to put in each column seems overwhelming. But life is full of accounting. Whether it is a child who is asked to explain his actions, an annual statement from the bank, or an employee held responsible for a company's productivity, accountability is a life principle.

Jesus told a story about a master and a servant in order to prepare His listeners for the most important day of accounting – Judgment Day. His message was full of good news for those who had listened with faith and believed who He was. Their acts of kindness would reflect the life of His Spirit within them, and He would invite them to come celebrate.

Lord,
Thank You that You have spoken words of life into my heart and my faith has grown. I want to offer my gifts back to You.
Amen.

December 31